LIVING HALFWAY

For the big brown dog.

I miss her.

And for the little yellow puppy.

Someday I will miss her, too.

This really happened.

*If present, past, and future break apart and bleed into one
as you read, consider that the light around you is sourced
from your present, reflected off the mirror of your past,
and bent through the lens of your future.*

*Where you are, where you've been, and where you want to be,
all influence what you see right now.*

*And if you're sensitive to offensive language, you should probably
go back to whatever you were doing a minute ago.*

ADMISSION

This book started out as a collection of rants from a foul-mouthed, 57-year-old chain-smoking lady living in a run-down trailer park.

She'd come to life in moments of vexed observation, when I'd notice irritating human behavior, but didn't want to do the actual complaining myself. I chose her voice because she was of the opposite sex and not at all with the times: she lived within her means, still called herself a waitress (instead of a 'server,' to the chagrin of those crazy chick-libbers she worked with) and had little aptitude for the digital age.

For reasons best left to a talented therapist's analysis, I began referring to this lady by my porn-star name. My skill-set, unfortunately, isn't well-suited to that particular branch of the film industry tree, so I employed a popular party trick and married the moniker of my first pet to that of my childhood street.

From the ragged aluminum stair serving as her front porch, Tweety Park bitched to her younger neighbor about the selfie-obsessed Instagram darling two doors down, the oblivious cell-phone user who almost ran her over, and the entitled jerk who left their plastic bag of dog waste by her trailer for the poop fairy to throw away. She'd make up new words on the spot, when whatever answers she'd learned on *Jeopardy* failed her, and hide dull pearls of hardscrabble wisdom in the grit of her monologues.

Tweety's neighbor, despite her more politically correct leanings, couldn't help but laugh at these often inappropriate, and occasionally explicit, takes on modern life. People who find fault in almost everything can be funny, like most successful, caustic comedians.

But are they happy?

I imagined Tweety's amused, yet concerned, neighbor inviting her next door to watch a video about how to manifest a better life. Tweety had already seen those quacks from 'The Secret' on *Oprah*, but reluctantly agreed, if only to get her woo-woo neighbor off her back. Midway through the video, Tweety realized the so-called 'thought-leader' was just trying to sell her most recent book, and abrasively decided that manifesting must be for pussies who didn't want to find a real job.

Tweety's words, not mine.

I started to love this lady, until I realized she was, kind of, well... me.

Then I got nervous.

I'd spent a few years buried in self-improvement culture, after my first published book inspired what would be the late, great Dr. Wayne Dyer's last book. He took me on the road with him,

8

this incredible grandfather of motivation, where I sang and spoke on stages I could only dream of stumbling across when I was chasing my music dream. He even invited me to perform on his last PBS special, and the words he whispered in my ear as I left the stage will stay with me forever.

Those beautiful memories float far above the leftover sludge I found in self-help-land's reedy swamp of bullshit, which teemed with the hypocrisy between many 'thought-leader' messages and the way they actually lived their lives. Wayne also noticed the sanctimonious posturing, and called it out amidst kind pleas for authenticity, until he died peacefully in his sleep on the island he loved.

I miss him.

Wayne's dawn ritual was to incant *thank you, thank you, thank you* the moment he got out of bed. Mine has become crushing wild sage between my fingers as I walk the game trail behind my small ranch, which reminds me to be grateful, especially when my sleepy head isn't quite there yet.

I was holding the fragrant remnants to my breath one recent morning when a huge bull moose emerged on the ridge. He looked through me for a few moments before dropping out of sight, as Wayne's wise, commanding, unmistakable baritone echoed across the canyon.

He said I'd better start speaking my truth.

And that lady in the trailer park?

She was part of it.

So, I followed the chain-smoking muse. I embraced her cussing, her brashness, her unapologetic struggle, until her story became my own, and our merged voices evolved into a tongue-in-cheek-titled book, penned by my alter-ego.

Manifesting is for Pussies by Tweety Park started exchanging hands, and readers were soon letting me know how deeply they saw themselves in the stories. They also told me that there's nothing like a book with *Pussies* in the title to require excessive, repentant explanations and disclaimers.

The farcical title suggested more of a misogynistic anti-self-help missive, rather than an offering of true stories about finding what works in life by discovering what doesn't... stories told with frustration, vulnerability, and honesty, by a man who broke down on the interstate to someday and left his dream car to rust on the shoulder. A man who settled in the nearest little has-been ghost town, where he started living halfway and...

Wait a minute.

Living Halfway.

That's a better title.

Still a whole lot of *fucks* running through this thing, though.

HELLO

Maybe you've recently puked up some ayahuasca in a Laurel Canyon VRBO, or dropped a half-hit of LSD at a tech-sponsored Burning Man camp, in an accelerated search for some sort of life-affirming wisdom you can't quite grasp.

Grasping anything of value can be tough sledding, especially when you have five fingers fumbling with the self-driving feature on your Tesla, and the other five holding your phone.

You're not alone.

Lonely, perhaps.

But not alone.

Many of us have grown tired of living halfway to someday, stalled out on popular culture's road, paved with impermanence and ultimately hollow promises. The social media age has only magnified this delusion of comparative happiness, and we desperately need a reset button, some sort of shift in awareness that will give the colors of our lives a deeper, truer vibrancy.

I say *you* and *we* and *us*, but who the fuck am I kidding?

This is about me.

SHITBAG

I'm a million miles away, floating along the western edge of the nature preserve down the street from my house, where the dawn mist clings to the willows and a soft sea wind blows dove melodies from the cottonwood trees.

Tribal legends have drifted for ten thousand years through these mystic reeds, rooted in the nourishing collision of fresh water from the coastal mountains and the saltwater bounty of the ocean. I've been gone from this place for a while, but now I drift here, too, in this confluence of ancient and personal history.

My fingers brush the waist-high grass as I breathe deep and walk moccasin-quiet through the early morning peace, daydreaming that instead of a reluctant warrior, I'm Russell Crowe at the end of *Gladiator*, brushing the same waist-high grass on a battle-weary return home to my beautiful family.

A self-composed cinematic theme song lifts this scene into the heavens of redemption, and I am triumph embodied, I am success realized, I am a dream come true and a lost love found, I am everything I thought I'd be by now, I am a crinkling, strained crunch under my right foot.

I stop mid-stride, and look down to discover a little pink piece of plastic peeking out from under my shoe.

But this isn't just any little pink piece of plastic.

This is a little pink plastic bag of dog shit.

Somebody has watched their precious LuLu take a dump, wrapped the waste in a little pink plastic bag, and left the accomplishment on the side of the trail.

Who does that?

I'll tell you who.

shitbag *(n) an individual bearing the marks of entitlement who wilts in the face of responsibility*

A shitbag.

Because I saw this same little pink plastic bag with the double-knot right here yesterday, and gave the depositing party the benefit of the doubt, hoping they'd pick the special delivery up on their way out.

But now I know they had no intention of coming back. They elected to abandon their shit for someone else to deal with. Maybe the burden was too heavy to carry, or they were worried they'd get a disease, although that Tinder swipe at the wine bar is likely a more reliable infectious option.

I have a lot of experience in this area.

Well, not in banging a Tinder swipe.

Everything about my old dog was big and brown, and I used to carry plastic bags of her substantial turds out of this nature preserve. The only transmission I ever encountered was a warmish palm, not exactly unwelcome on chilly walks, but the pebbles in this bag are rock-hard cold from being left outside overnight.

Shitbags must have some sort of strength in numbers, which makes them feel better about leaving their shit for other people to deal with. I've been seeing little pink, black, brown and green plastic bags lurking everywhere, from the side of this trail to the beach, sidewalk and riverbank. I even saw one hanging from a tree last week, like a Christmas turd ornament.

I pick up as many of those bags as my small hands and matchstick forearms will hold, carry them wherever they need to go, and throw them away. Like I'm doing right now.

Imagine the world if we all dealt with our own shit, instead of packaging it up pretty and leaving it for someone else to deal with.

I'm talking about life here, shitbag.

And your little pink plastic bag of shit.

COCKSTROKE

This stretch of wetlands opens to a wide beach bordering the Pacific, where wave after traveling wave waited at sunrise to grace my feet, at the end of their own thousand-some mile journey. Rolling salt water buckets offered to wash away the sand clinging to my jeans, gray t-shirt, and every inch of exposed skin, but I was runnniiinnnngggggg.

Partly because I fell asleep on the beach last night. But mostly because when you leave on the back of a magic flying dragon, a majestic beast with talons of tenacity and wings of promise, and return in the rump of a Lyft driver's Corolla two decades and a buried friend later, that's what you do.

runnnniiiinnnnggggggg *(v)*
movement popularized by
Forrest Gump, in which taking
steps anywhere is valued over
taking steps nowhere

You run, with the ghost of a young dog galloping through the surf, across these same grains of eroded earth that cushioned hopeful steps a dream ago.

You run, because you believe in Forrest Gump under the Spanish moss. You can hear Jenny yelling *Run Forrest, Run!* as you sprint down the dirt road next to him, as the gravel dissolves to sand, as you become one, as the metal and springs and bullies and bullshit holding you back disintegrate, until you run into the rest of your life, across the Alabama football field, through the deserts and mountains, and into everyone's hearts.

That may not be you, but I wanted that to be me.

And I may have taken flight over these reeds on a mythic dragon, but I now stand before a very different beast, with talons of thievery and wings of decline, circling my mom's sky in a cruel waning twilight. Ever since the claws of dementia have tightened their grip, she whipsaws between two extremes, abrasively judging everything around her, while lightly caressing my back like she used to do when I was sick in bed with an underdeveloped immune system.

I pull in a breath heavy with ocean mist, turn away from the coast, and head deeper into the wetlands.

Nothing like coming home to find out how far I haven't come.

I'm assaulted on my exhale by a brash, excited voice, bouncing against the static of an AM-radio wall and thundering down the trail like a steam train. A bearded hipster in skinny jeans and a denim jacket brushes past me, looking straight down at his phone.

Stroking it with his thumb.

Except he's not only stroking it, he's talking to somebody on speakerphone at the same time, so the trees and I can hear about the sweet deal he's making on a Tesla Model X.

I don't know why he's so excited. Of all things to seek approval for, he's slobbering over being allowed to rent a six-figure glorified soccer-mom minivan masquerading as a sport-utility vehicle, which he'll never actually own and doesn't do anything utility, especially short on battery a hundred miles from a charging station.

I'd rather have a Tesla jam on the jukebox than on the freeway.

Remember that band?

Signs, signs, everywhere the signs.

Here's a sign. Of demise.

This guy with a pomaded dome and well-coiffed facial hair has his head at a right angle to his body, stroking and over-talking on his California-designed but Chinese-made iPhone, mindlessly flailing through a space that resonates with traces of the sacred.

Deer sleep in these wetlands, hawks circle this sky, an ancient riverbed empties into that sparkling ocean, and he's stomping blindly through this beautiful sliver of nature, blathering about a composite of metal and wires and batteries and rubber that's waaaayyyyyy better for the environment.

Hey! Watch where the fuck you're going!

He looks up mid-cockstroke, like a startled chipmunk with his nuts in his hand.

cockstroke *(v) to engage in a selfish act of disrespect for one's self or surroundings*

Yeah YOU.

I wave him past me, shaking my head and muttering under my breath.

Fuck.

These phones make us think we're connected.

I don't know about you, but I don't stroke it when I'm connected.

Only when I'm lonely.

MASSAGERBATE

The hipster's denim backside disappears into the trees, and I head back down the trail, absently tripping over a small wooden bridge spanning a run-off ditch. I catch myself from falling as the first flash of harsher daylight spreads across the reeds, silencing the crickets' post-dawn reveille.

Abrupt quiet marries momentary weightlessness, opening a door sealed against the rattle and hum of my near constant mental chatter. A sacred door, into a beat-up Chevrolet running an empty high-desert interstate, with Glenn Frey behind the wheel, Prince next to him, and Tom Petty in the backseat with me, singing "Already Gone" under a cloudless sky.

Dead legends and me, riding into the mystic.

I don't expect to see her standing there when I regain my footing. She's leaning casually against a cottonwood tree, her thick, dark hair framing a flawless visage, luminous with the sunlight filtering through the branches, and into the deep pond reflection of her eyes.

She's perfect.

Too perfect to be out here, especially this early in the morning.

But I love her.

Ever since I sprouted my first tardy pubic hair, I've been drawn to women who embody some quality I actually want to manifest in myself. This one has a manicured beauty that eludes me, but I'm also missing confidence, a free spirit, and an unexamined, unconditional social admiration.

The list of what I'm not, but find attractive in others, is exhaustive. And exhausting.

I figured this out a couple of years ago, when I was wondering why I'd inexplicably bailed on a perfectly adequate relationship. I wrote down a list of everything I wanted in a girlfriend, hoping that I'd find the break-up reason next to whatever box my ex didn't check off. She checked-off every single box, but something was still missing, which is how I realized I was looking at a must-have list for myself.

This future girlfriend, and wife, and mother of my children, with her back against the tree in the nature preserve… she might be different.

Maybe she's the one.

I'm sorting through my mental inventory of introductory excuses when she pulls her phone out of her front pocket, holds it at arm's length, tilts her head, hits a button, and checks the screen.

There's my answer.

I'll offer to take a photo for her.

I take a hesitant step forward as she flips her hair and repeats the process.

Repeat.

Repeat.

I take no more steps forward.

Repeat.

She tucks her hair up into a hey-I'm-casual-but-cute bun, with purposely placed strands of hair brushing her cheeks.

Repeat.

Smiles smaller.

Repeat.

Doesn't smile, looks pouty.

That's the one.

She wastes a minute doing the cockstroke, presumably filtering and editing until her image looks perfect. Or at least better than the competition.

And with a final stroke, she sends her curated self into the ether. I know, because I can see the Instagram profile on her screen as I trudge by. She already has more hearts for her selfie than I have people who would notice if I disappeared.

I chose Teddy Roosevelt for an extra-credit report in 4th grade, mostly because I saw a picture of him on a horse in one of my dad's books about dead presidents. After consulting the Encyclopedia Britannica my mom gave me for Christmas, Mr. Roosevelt and I seemed to have a couple of key things in common.

He was a small, sickly kid, like I was. And he didn't like math.

What he did next with his life reverberated with the triumph I dreamed I could embody someday, before life got in the way. He graduated from Harvard, led the Rough Riders through the Spanish-American war, became Governor of New York, Vice-President of the United States, and President of the United States, received the Nobel Peace Prize, and now his face is on Mount Rushmore. My extra-credit report started with one of his observations.

Comparison is the thief of joy.

He probably wasn't comparing himself to anyone else because he was too busy doing awesome shit, like establishing the United States Forest Service, signing into law the creation of five National Parks, and protecting over 230 million acres, including nature preserves a lot like this one.

With you in mind, so you can massagerbate reality into a fake perfect photo of yourself and compare the vapid reactions to other perfect photos and vapid reactions, instead of noticing the beauty all around you.

massagerbate (v)
to manipulate in a self-serving way. See also: massage, masturbate

And me.

I wish I could've told you how the sunlight filtered through the branches into the deep pond reflection of your eyes.

But you were so busy making yourself look perfect.

And I'm kind of a wuss, anyway.

ROCKSTAR

A hard wind rips through the nature preserve, forcing tired leaves to abandon their trusted cottonwood branches and spiral toward a late autumn bed of moss, twigs and sticks. Fall bleeds into Christmas around here, where the price for nice weather is an anemic change in seasons.

I used to revel in quiet joy when I found sticks like these, clutching them in my tiny hands as I ran through the cold late afternoons and chimney smoke of my childhood. The thin, wooden light sabers warded off imagined evils lurking in the trees, on my quest to save the galaxy and restore the Force.

I ran through those days like they were forever, like there would always be another stick, until I found myself in the metal, glass and asphalt of adulthood, where make-believe sword-sticks are swept away by loud trucks with unforgiving brushes. Saving the galaxy and restoring the Force has been reduced to bitching at three minor societal offenders in a fifty yard span. One heard me, one didn't, and one wasn't even there.

And now, I just want to go back to finding sticks again.

I sit against the trunk of a thick, experienced matriarch, pick up one of the smaller branches laying in the crook of an exposed root, and search each strand of the tree's tired, fibrous hair for a way back to what used to be. Following one leaf's descent to earth, my eyes grow heavier and breath steadier with each faint floating flutter, the pictures moving with deepening vibrancy behind my eyes.

Her life cycles in slow-motion, a new green bud of spring promise blossoming into a robust cauldron of summer sunlight, a photosynthetic creator of energy fading to a reluctant autumn hanger-on. And now, her spiral contrail weaves into those of her comrades, like wool on the loom, until the leaves circle in a slow rain, a lazy fall hurricane with a calm eye, inviting me to step inside.

I push to my feet and duck into the soft storm, pausing in the shaft of sunlight granted access from above, to let my gaze drift across the inner fall tapestry. But in here, there are no yellows or oranges or deep reds. In here, the leaves are square pieces of stubborn paper, swirling in suspension, images blurred in the dun.

I reach a tentative hand into the fray and pull the first photograph that touches my index finger into the light. The subtle outline of a small boy with a guitar deepens into an almost-realized picture, until my younger, blonder, still-there mom is sitting opposite me, with her camera on our shag living room floor. I'm barely able to walk, but completely able to bang on my sister's nylon-strung guitar with a tiny fist, smiling through a chorus of toddler angst. Because even then, there's a felt, unsaid magic in creating something, where before there was nothing.

Something unlistenable, perhaps.

But something.

I throw the guitar onto the carpet and stumble over to the piano, where I reach as high as my stubby arms will allow, to hit the keys with clumsy elbows, until my mom pulls me away to save both her patience and the inherited family instrument.

I will come back to this same piano and guitar for the rest of my life, when I need a friend with whom to cry or contemplate. I will ask this piano and guitar to support me, to give me a career and a family and a connection to others I can't forge with talk of small things.

But I will never ask for this simple joy again.

BATMAN

I tuck the photograph into my jeans pocket, as another undeveloped Polaroid drifts into my periphery. Shepherding the picture further into the light, I wait for the unfocused lines to sharpen, until a small boy emerges wearing a cheap, black plastic mask and petting a tiny white dog.

I'm in my grandma's kitchen before kindergarten on Halloween morning, dressed in Batman flannel pajamas and a homemade blue nylon cape. My mom doesn't want to pay for the real costume that comes in a box at the drugstore, because she's already bought me jammies at JC Penney that will work *just fine*, so we're showing my outfit to my grandma on our way to school.

An unabashed grin is plastered on my face as my mom takes a picture of me crouched next to my grandma's poodle. I tell anybody who will listen, including myself, that her dog is mine, because I'm free, alive and invincible, whenever I'm with her.

My mom won't let me have a dog, so my first and likely only

pet is a finch named Tweety, which my sister rescued over the weekend from the pool behind our house at 291 Park Avenue. My mom set up a cage next to the den window, so Tweety can look outside at the freedom he'll never know again. I feed the bird every morning, swap the pooped-on newspaper for a clean sports section every night, and tell him that someday he's going to fly again.

Yesterday I came home from kindergarten to discover that his brownish feathers had transformed in a matter of hours to snow white. And thus begins my oft-repeated, ill-informed, and self-told story about how a caged, wild bird had in fact grown more beautiful in captivity.

I won't be informed for two decades that my mom has slyly swapped out the dead finch she'd found on the bottom of the cage that morning with a pet-store replacement, sparing both of us the uncomfortable talk about how everything dies. She could've had Springsteen explain death to me on the 8-track in the living room, which is sort of what my dad will do when the time comes to have the other uncomfortable talk. He'll give me a *Penthouse* and a *Playboy* and tell me to let him know if I have any questions.

I'll have many, none of which I'll ask.

Anyway, my grandma's little poodle and I are exhausted from playing hide-and-seek through the cavernous rooms of her house, and we're now tangled in a boy-and-dog joyful mess on the kitchen linoleum. I laugh and shriek as my mom pulls me by one arm off the floor and drags me away, so she won't be late for work and I won't be late for kindergarten.

I'm basking in dog glow as I walk into the classroom, but my heart sinks when I see that most of the other kids are wearing real costumes from the drugstore. A couple of boys even have the same Batman outfit I'd wanted.

I watch the clock until recess, follow the rest of Mrs. Bryant's class to the playground, and join the single file line to parade around in front of the whole elementary school. The stream of kindergartners loses momentum by the tetherball court, and a weird quiet falls over the playground, as the birds stop chirping, the kids stop talking, and the teachers stop directing traffic.

I don't have to look up from my Keds to know that everybody is staring at me, the little towhead with his pajamas on. An older kid calls out *Is that supposed to be a cape* and somebody starts chanting the theme song to *Batman*, my favorite show on TV. Except they're sort of taunting the melody, not singing with heart, like I do.

I close my eyes and try not to listen, pretending these invisible lasers can't burn through the thin blue fabric of the cape.

I'm Batman.

Nothing can hurt me.

Until a searing burn cuts across my neck and wrists, the nylon straps breaking away under an immediate, violent pressure. I turn around in time to see David Schultz, who's already been

30

held back a year, push aside the little girl behind me on his way to the playground, where he stripper-twirls between his legs the fabric that my mom spent late hours after work hemming and stitching.

The little girl wraps herself around me in a protective bear hug, as a single laugh from somewhere in the fourth grade line spreads through to the sixth graders, and now all I can hear is laughter mixed with taunts, all I can see are fingers pointed at me, and all I can feel is something I don't recognize, pushing and pulling in my stomach.

Something that will keep me in my room most afternoons, where nobody can laugh or taunt or point their fingers at me again, unless that finger is a light saber in the plastic hand of a prized Star Wars action figure. I don't yet know what to call that something, but this kindergarten sucker punch gives me the same tightness in my stomach that my mom's disapproval will give me down the road.

Christmas morning later that year, she'll intonate *Damnyou* through clenched teeth, after my new X-Wing fighter's stubborn wheels leave a scratch in the linoleum, and I'll start calling this something *Damnyou*.

The little girl lets go and I drop my chin to my chest, which makes my tears easier to swallow. Mrs. Bryant wrestles the cape away from David Schultz and gives it back to me before the parade line moves, but I'll never tie those nylon straps to my wrists again.

Not even that night for Halloween.

When I tell my mom that afternoon why I'm not going trick or treating, she asks why not.

It's just a Halloween costume.

X-WING

The crinkling of crushed laminated paper startles me back into the revolving autumn darkroom, where I've wrapped my fingers so tightly around this precious photograph that the edges have become crumpled and torn. I relax my grip and coax this reminder of joy, this moment before *Damnyou* was born, into the first photograph's denim cocoon, and watch the Polaroid whirlwind begin to circle slower.

Slow.

Slo.

Sl.

S.

A picture lands heart-level, offering only a necktie resting on a starched, white button-down shirt. I reach a tentative hand across the chasm and press the memory against my thumb with a trembling index finger, because I already know where this image will take me, I already know I haven't been to that beautiful place in years, I already know there's no one else to blame, I already know the nervous non-smile on the youngster's face, I already am standing defiantly in front of an open garage.

The metal of the clip-on tie is digging into the sensitive skin under my Adam's apple, forcing a scowl of resultant wince and subsequent choke from the pressure of the top-buttoned collar. This is the last night I'll have to wear this tie, and I'm posed here so my mom can visually immortalize my pre-pubescent handsomeness.

School had barely started this past September when my mom saw a flyer for something called Cotillion posted on the bulletin board at our neighborhood church, where she'd enrolled me in a faith-based after-school program. She bleeds an atheism that questions what kind of God would leave her in a Masonic home until high school, but the promise of moral grounding is why I make crafts and learn about Jesus three afternoons a week now.

And why she ignored my backseat protests in the JC Penny parking lot last September, dragged me into the store, and bought me this clip-on tie, gray slacks, and blue blazer.

And also why, instead of our Monday Night Football ritual hangout with Howard Cosell and Frank Gifford, my dad has been dropping me off at the church assembly hall, where I'm supposed to learn how to dance the foxtrot, make appropriate conversation, eat cookies and drink punch.

I fucking hate punch.

But not as much as learning how to ask girls to dance, which is like learning how to gouge my own eyes out. I can hardly find my breath, let alone intelligible words, whenever I approach the foreign objects sitting on the girls' side of the room. *Damnyou* dependably stirs in my stomach, sending buckets of sweat into my palms and forcing my heart to thump faster with each hesitant step.

Faking a bathroom emergency worked once, but not twice. And ever since the director caught me waiting out Cotillion in a stall, my foxtrot choice has been Alexis Lovejoy. I know she'll say yes, because I've been asking her to dance every Monday night since the beginning of this awful rite of suburban passage. She's a couple of heads taller than me, and having my face pushed against her washboard chest has become an increasingly welcome price for approaching her.

But I never, ever, ever approach Jenny Cooper.

She's perfect.

She's bloomed early, and although we've hardly aged out of our first decade, she already wears a relatively unnecessary bra and knows how to put on lip-gloss. I've heard she's dating a thirty-year-old, which is impressive considering she's barely twelve, and also all I need to know.

These Monday nights usually end at the lowest point imaginable, with a girls-ask-boys dance. Sometimes Alexis will swoop me up in a retaliatory move, but most of the time, I'm among the last ones chosen on the boys' side of the room.

I'm short, shy, and young for my grade, with a conscience that keeps me a Star Wars galaxy away from being cool, which is why I have to hear third-hand the stories of what goes on behind the building at recess. That's where the elementary school elite light the wicks on M-80s and their futures, while kissing each other in contests timed with Casio stopwatches.

Also, last week I suffered a sudden expulsion from indifferent inclusion on this very dance floor. David Schultz, whose terrorizing of the defenseless has helped him become the most popular boy in our grade, was dancing with Jenny Cooper when he reached over and ripped off my clip-on tie. He'd proclaimed victory between hoots, holding my tie like a scalp, in the same fist he'd gripped my homemade cape back in kindergarten.

Damnyou reached up from my stomach again that night, snatched my heart with unforgiving claws, and pulled down hard. Most of the kids who'd laughed at my Batman jammies costume in kindergarten had regressed into committed disciples of David Schultz, following him here to Cotillion. They looked to him for direction, then piled head-first onto the clip-on-tie scrum.

So, the chances of anybody, male or female, choosing to dance with me are slim to none. An interminable few seconds have passed since the girls were directed to proposition the boys, and even Alexis isn't coming my way. I'm staring down the line of chairs at the other boys, watching each one peel off into the arms of decreasing validation, when the most beautiful voice I've ever heard floats past my left side and into the textured drywall.

Would you like to dance with me?

I immediately look down at the tiny hands in my lap, since the question is obviously for the lucky bastard sitting next to me. His feet start to move in apparent agreement, but the words sound again, this time with a hint of gentle amusement.

Would you like to dance with me?

Two fingers float into the frame, landing on my left wrist, and I lift my gaze, squinting into a fluorescent halo surrounding an impossible angel.

Jenny Cooper.

She takes my hand and leads me to the center of the room, where we assume the proper Cotillion position, and box-step through a circle of light usually reserved for moments in my sister's favorite Molly Ringwald movies.

I never want the song to end. I never want my life to end. I never want anything to ever end.

Ever.

Because right now, I'm Luke Skywalker's co-pilot in an X-Wing fighter.

Jenny moves her fingers across my shoulder and the spaceship dives in a breathless drop, until she presses into my palm and the rocket ship banks right, until her exhale brushes past my neck and the X-wing accelerates up into the heavens, on a mission to destroy the Death Star of not-even-adolescent-yet hell, manned by David Schultz.

And I live inside every single sweaty special awkward moment, as if this beautiful scene in space and time might never come again.

The song does end, despite my silent offer of conversion to whatever religion necessary to keep the tired waltz spilling out of the speakers. A voice booms through the room telling us to go home and Jenny pulls me closer, touches the fabric clipped to my collar, and whispers *I like your tie.*

I search my shoes for the right thing to say, but by the time I look up she's gone, absorbed into the crowd of everyone I will never know, everything I will never understand, and everywhere I will never belong.

I fly out of the assembly hall doors and sprint to the line of cars, where my dad is waiting in the coupe he only drives on weekends and special occasions. He smiles as I collapse into the front seat, take off my clip-on tie, and stuff it in my blazer pocket.

What happened to you? You alright?

Jenny Cooper happened to me.

I won one.

You alright?

A thin voice drops from the ether and I self-consciously shove the Cotillion photo into my jeans, the quiet hurricane of leaves around me falls to the ground, and my eyes flutter open.

The hipster must be on his way back through the nature preserve, because he's kneeling next to me, craning his neck so he can get a better look at my face.

Hey man, you alright?

I smile sheepishly and nod. He looks down thoughtfully toward my hip, decides against whatever question he was going to ask, and evaporates down the trail.

I reach into my jeans pocket to make sure the photos aren't scrunched into a ruinous bundle, but all my fingers find is a warm, squishy mound of plastic, and all my tired eyes see is a pink double-knot, peeking out from the depths of denim fabric.

Who puts a bag of shit in their pocket?

CLOSETED

The opening flare of harsher daylight slashes across the reeds, the sundial blaze reminding me I have a plane to catch this afternoon, so I can play a throwaway gig halfway across the country tomorrow night.

I hustle out of the nature preserve, drop the bag in the trashcan by the road, and walk-then-jog the couple hundred yards to my dirt driveway. The ancient, gnarled pepper trees lining the long approach are dry with neglect, begging for the precious fresh water subject to draconian drought restrictions.

If it hasn't rained enough, the Chicken Littles come out to play. And work. And legislate. If it *has* rained enough, news anchors complain about their ruined weekends.

Sometimes, when the irrigation police are tucked away in their lonesome beds, I connect two hoses together, turn on the spigot, and rotate a slow drip to quench the parched roots' thirst. I'll be traveling for a few days, so in broad daylight and at risk of potential flogging, I leave water trickling at the base of the closest pepper, and slip through the side entry into the closed garage.

This pro-life-yet-slightly-against-the-rules move elicits a predictable reaction, as *Damnyou's* creeping tendrils push open an imaginary door into the punitive internal broom closet my mom started building for me when I was in kindergarten.

Unversed in the vagaries of financial markets, I'd happily pocketed a toy helicopter at JC Penney while she was paying for my Halloween Batman jammies. She noticed the unfamiliar bulge in my front pocket on the way to the car, dug her fingernails into my forearm, dragged me back into the store, and oversaw my confused apology to the manager for a rule violation I didn't understand.

Catching my tear-stained eyes in the rearview mirror as we pulled out of the parking lot, she told me in simpler words that rules, especially those enjoying omnipotence with limited explanation, made the world go around. She'd learned this in foster care at a Masonic home, where if she didn't make her bed with hospital corners or finish every speck of food on her plate, she'd be sentenced to the dank confines of the broom closet. And while she'd never actually been in there, she'd heard third-hand stories of hours spent in the straight-backed wooden chair that might as well have had leather wrist straps and a voltage meter.

This broom closet sounded a lot like hell, which I'd prematurely discovered the week before in Sunday School. The gently foreboding preacher-teacher had used colorful illustrations to promise eternal damnation if I strayed from a rule-paved path I'd neither chosen, nor could see. Terrified, I'd readily offered biblical-picture-book compliance, so I could vaguely relate to this broom closet concept of fear-based deference to threat.

41

By the time she unbuckled my seatbelt in the garage, my mom had unintentionally convinced me that a driving factor in her life was avoidance of the broom closet, which over the course of a JC Penny trip, had rapidly devolved into building one for me to avoid.

At all costs.

And even now, whenever I engage in behavior even slightly against the rules, *Damnyou* conspires with the broom closet to coax me into the subtle better-not-get-caught walls, still standing decades later, thanks to the strong foundation of Ivory soap bars my mom favored for construction.

One of the first white bricks was set soon after Roger Staubach threw his only pick in Super Bowl XIII. My dad muttered a barely intelligible disapproval into his can of Budweiser, and the violent echo of my first contextually understood cuss word loosened a hidden hinge in the paneled den wall, revealing a forbidden, glorious linguistic chamber. Now I knew where my dad went on Sundays when he watched football. Semantically speaking, of course.

I wanted to join him, but because cussing was a major broom closet affair at home, I worked on the delivery behind my closed bedroom door for months, waiting for my opportunity to test the word's playground efficacy. The agony of a final defeat on the tetherball court to David Schultz during the last week of school was buffered by the awe-struck approval of the kids waiting to take on the winner, and I'd suddenly found my new favorite form of self-expression.

My mom found out, even though she'd been at work. Somehow

she found out about everything, and when I got home that afternoon, she suggested near-death-experiences every time I tried to interject an explanatory protest. Only upon meekly acquiesced guilt did she give me not even an actual choice: either I had absolutely no chance of going to Disneyland the next day for my birthday, or I was getting a bar of Ivory soap shoved between my teeth.

I'd spent a year's worth of Saturday mornings fudging my painfully slow growth progress with a pencil and ruler on my bedroom wall. And by my current calculations, I was finally tall enough to ride Space Mountain.

So, I squeezed my eyes shut tight, fought back the tears, and gagged on the glycerin, which was supposed to clean out every last streak of filth in my mouth. But that was a PacMan-Laser-Disc-PrettyInPink-SixteenCandles-DeLorean-MTV-LikeAVirgin-long-ass-time-ago, when the promise of tomorrow felt less like a mold-stricken bathtub half-empty with tepid water, and more like a Four Seasons jacuzzi steaming with strippers.

Or Disneyland, if I played my cards right and got out of the broom closet.

I spat the soap out as soon as my mom deemed the lesson learned, muttering under my breath the same cuss word I got in trouble for in the first place. I didn't even learn the intended lesson. All I really learned from being closeted was to avoid confrontation and internalize emotion.

You must unlearn what you have learned.

This timely and not-yet-able-to-be-conceptualized suggestion

43

arrived later that night, after my mom and dad went to bed and I snuck downstairs to escape into *The Empire Strikes Back* on the VHS player. About halfway through the movie, Luke Skywalker's X-wing fighter started sinking into the swamp of Dagobah. He was understandably vexed about losing the spaceship that could take him on galaxy-saving adventures, and thought he couldn't raise the glorious hunk of steel from the mire by himself. Yoda told Luke that this learned belief was only true in his mind.

You must unlearn what you have learned.

Luke agreed to try, but Yoda shook his head.

No. Try not. Do. Or do not. There is no try.

Luke, Princess Leia, C3PO and R2D2 watched Lando Calrissian take off in the Millennium Falcon in search of Han Solo, and I went to bed. I stared at the red digital numbers on the alarm clock for an hour, wondering if Yoda had ever tried to find his way out of a closet, because I was definitely trying in the name of Disneyland, and my mom had made clear nothing was guaranteed.

Not that Yoda was gay. I mean, maybe he was gay. But 'gay' was an old-timey word for 'happy,' back when I didn't know that particular type of closet existed. Not that gay people aren't happy. They just aren't the only ones with closets. Never mind. I'm having trouble saying what I mean.

As my own X-wing fighter sinks quietly behind me, into the apathetic swamp of this garage.

I CAN PACK YOUR ASS

I feel my way across the half-light of unpainted drywall in the concrete purgatory for what shouldn't be left outside, but isn't yet allowed in, this halfway point dependent on unreliable white tubes of illumination. Hitting the switch for the overhead fluorescent bulb, I stumble over one of the cardboard boxes laying in wait for the great spark-joy purge that will probably never happen. The tired container responds with a thud as she tips over, her insides scattering across the garage floor.

Stark white flickers to life over some yearbooks, a wilted clump of flowers, a clip-on tie, and my blue Batman cape from kindergarten. I apologetically nudge the box upright, take a knee to usher the artifacts back to their hiding place, and pause over the junior high *Mustang Memories*, tumbled open to a page with scrawled handwriting.

I wonder why I let these cardboard boxes, taped at weathered seams of the past, take up any space at all.

Just grow. - Jeff

I can't see you because you're too short. GROW. Have a bitchen summer anyway. - Greg

Too bad you can't surf or I'd invite you to Trestles with me. Too bad you wimped out on Jr. Guards. - Bob

And of course, this brilliant missive from David Schultz.

> Youre a dick
> yoore to short, and
> you have umetal
> mouth, youre
> weak at basket
> because I can
> Kick your
> ass

You know what they say, about how people only give other people shit because they love them?

That's a lie.

Words matter.

AAA

Mustang Memories slips through my jaded fingers, as if feigned indifference will translate into actual letting go, and falls with a thud to the floor. I have semi-better things to do before I leave later this afternoon, including a Trader Joe's run for cereal, pasta, and airplane snacks, and the music store for a guitar tuner.

I open the overhead garage door and climb into Princess Leia. Not the person, although that would be my first crush dream come true. She may be gone from this earth, but she's immortalized in film, and her name will be tattooed on the hearts of guys like me until we're gone, too.

This Leia is my Chevy Duramax. She's carried me through rain, snow, sleet and heat, to the never-surrender soundtrack of Springsteen satellite radio. Killing her via dome light is no way to thank her, and I spend a half-minute torquing the key in the ignition, but her engine isn't turning over.

The AAA guy has her breathing minutes after he arrives, and tells me that if I give her some time to recharge, she'll be fine.

All I have crumpled in my jeans pocket is a twenty-dollar bill, but when I try to tip him, he tells me to pay it forward.

I ask him what that means, and he raises his eyebrows.

You ever seen the movie called 'Pay It Forward' with the Sixth Sense kid?

Nope. But I haven't seen *The Graduate* either, and I've heard it's about me.

Do something nice for somebody else, and that'll be enough of a tip for me. Looks like that tree is good on water, by the way.

Tree?

Oh.

I run down the driveway and shut off the hose drip, which has flooded the tree well, and walk back to thank the AAA guy. He's already behind the sealed window glass of his truck door, engine running, truck moving.

I'm already behind Leia's wheel, engine running, truck moving.

He's already leaving a trail of dry dust over the driveway.

We're already banking in opposite directions.

And, having met briefly in time like so many other random, anonymous crossings that offer more than we appreciate in the moment, already passing on to the rest of our lives.

48

TEXT-GAP

Some hundred feet later, I roll to a stop behind an Audi buffered by a text-gap. I peer through the A4's rear window at a cell
phone, aglow with the blue border of a Face-
book page, just as the driver spreads his index
and middle fingers across the screen to en-
large the filtered image of a bikini-clad coed.

text-gap *(n)*
distance between
cars necessary
for phone
messaging
and social
media activity

I can see a lot from this Duramax, and sometimes it's not a phone they're stroking.

His flat-billed hat nods either in approval, or in time with the
bass thundering from his trunk. I check my side mirror, where
an early 1980s Toyota pickup, with rakes and shovels lashed precariously to its flank, is much closer than it appears. The Audi's
cyclone of low-end drowns out the landscape guy's screaming
frustration, so he resorts to an accusatory shake of both hands,
motioning me forward in between staccato trumpet beeps.

Albeit satisfying, monster-trucking-it over the shitbag in front
of me may prove to be a life-threatening and lawsuit-inducing

course of action. Instead, I search my reactive internal toolbox for the small, petty opportunity to unload a deeper frustration likely unrelated to driving.

My fist is en route to Leia's horn when the Audi leaps into gear, instantaneously erasing the text-gap, before slamming to a sudden halt. This cat-and-shitbag game unfolds all the way to the intersection, where the road widens into a boulevard. We're at a signal now, and I'm guessing that as soon as the light changes to green, he'll be Froggering in between cars and pedestrians at a speed inversely related to his penis size.

A tiny tuft of hair pokes up from his backseat. That poor dog is probably relieved to be sitting upright, and not collapsed in a canine crumple between the seats. Almost every dog I see lately leaves me longing for what used to be, as if my golden era opened with a big, brown dog's arrival, and ended the afternoon she left.

I was boarding an airplane 2500 miles away when I got the call that she was missing. Five hours later I midnight-trolled the pond in front of the house, an hour after that I printed up flyers, and at first light I stapled her name, face, and phone number to every telephone pole within a mile of the house.

She was sleeping at my feet by mid-morning, thanks to a kind woman who rescued her from the middle of the road and managed to get her hundred dead-weight pounds into her car. She'd hobbled a half-mile with debilitating arthritis, a fused spine, an artificial hip, and two replaced knees to find me, after being left outside by the house-sitter.

She knew.

Two days passed before she couldn't come to me anymore. Her spirit was vibrant, her eyes bright and alert, but her body was failing by the minute. I told her I loved her, which she already knew, because I'd left no doubt over the last 13 years. I thanked her for showing me how to live with unrelenting joy, energy, and heart, and that I would carry her fight with me. I whispered that I hoped she'd find a wide open stretch of sand wherever she was going, and she could show it to me someday.

And she went down swinging.

Don't know what you got 'til it's gone.

Overdramatized, clichéd, and totally true, especially when couched in the bombastic '80s power ballad of the same name by Cinderella. 'Gypsy Road' was the third song on that cassette, which I rewound over and over on my way to high school every morning, until I could nail the blank tape space before the intro by feel. I'd pull into the gravel parking lot, the monster guitar riff offering immunity from the mocking glares of the cool kids listening to The Cure on their Sony Walkmen.

I still drive all night, just to see the light, but my gypsy road can't take me home.

They don't make bands like that anymore.

I don't think they make dogs like this, either, unless some new breed can bang a sippy-cup against the window, in an understandable attempt to break free from a death cauldron of computerized drum machine swill. This guy is checking out digital titties while driving like a *Fast and Furious* fanboy, with a toddler strapped to a plastic chair behind him.

The signal changes, he looks at his phone for a couple more seconds, and flies away as predicted, over the road's gentle rise and out of sight. I ease Leia into the intersection, touching her brakes when a flash of chrome in her side mirror temporarily blinds me.

No way.

This can't be happening.

It's Ponch.

From CHiPs.

He shines his gleaming, clean-shaven smile, gives me a thumbs up, and points in the direction of the shitbag.

He must think I'm Jon.

But I'm not Jon.

Fuck it, I'm Jon.

We accelerate over the hill and Ponch overtakes the Audi, his lights flashing and sirens sounding in concert with the glorious fury of our theme song's pulsing synthesizers. He motions for me to make sure the dude can't throw it in reverse and peel away, so I stay close to the Audi's bumper.

Until I put my left turn signal on, slowly move into the other lane, and drive by the entourage at a respectable crawl, as the heavyset mustached cop pulls the Audi over to the shoulder. I crane my neck long enough to see that the kid in the backseat is holding the phone, which the shitbag must have thrown at her in desperation.

Long enough to see that the kid is a cute blonde girl, about two years old.

Long enough for her to look up at me, smile and wave the phone.

Long enough for me to wonder what my life would have looked like if I'd had a daughter.

And long enough to crawl into the coiffed wisps of the shitbag's beard, swaying in the coastal breeze.

They grow a lot of those beards down here by the beach.

I don't know why.

Nobody needs a beard by the beach.

HOT MOM

Holy shit.

A brawl.

These two ladies are scratching across plumped lips and pulling at straightened strands of hair attached to trucker hats, splashed with brands aligned against their suburban lives. The brunette's clean, straight-billed John Deere billboard just got knocked off her curated head by the tan, moisturized fist of her blonde-ish challenger. But she doesn't even notice, because she's tearing apart her adversary's Lululemon outfit with slashing, manicured nails.

This uncaged match is heading toward blood, to the perverse delight of the afternoon crowd that's gathered to watch, when an impatient voice brings the snarling to an abrupt halt.

Ma'am.

MA'AM.

You can pay now.

All I wanted was some cereal, pasta, and snacks for the airplane at Trader Joe's. But now all I want is permission to slug the two uniformed hot moms holding court in line at adjacent cash registers.

I'm not really going to slug them, okay? The only time I'd probably slug anybody would be if they were messing with my own mom, and they'd deserve more of a beatdown than these little hands could deliver.

I love Trader Joe's. Customers here are encouraged to bag their own inexpensive, yet delicious, boxes of granola and bottles of wine. You know, handle their own shit.

Unfortunately, one of my neighborhood's great socioeconomic injustices revolves around this very store, where the Whole Foods contingency has inexplicably infected the aisles. The aristocracy in front of me can't be bothered with such plebeian nonsense as handling their own shit, at least not when they're botox deep in discourse about what vodka drink was at the Evanstons' pool party, and where Sienna's tiny cocktail dress came from, because it was soooooooo cute.

The checkout guys behind both registers are doing their best to scan and bag the mountains of crap piled into the shopping carts, but the growing lines behind these social diplomats are grumbling louder with each change of gossip topic. A bell rings, and two more crew members come over to help finish bagging what appears to be half of the store. We, as a people, are relieved.

Except the hot moms. They can't stop talking over each other in a rapidly escalating fuzz-bump battle, now being waged in the fertile soil of Facebook, where Maria looks so much *bigger* in her new photos.

Ma'am.

MA'AM.

You can pay now.

The checkout guy comes around the counter, stands in between them, and says *MA'AM* again, a little louder, with enough hint of annoyance to make the rest of us smile.

I'm trying to picture the men married to these nightmares, which reminds me that I'm still not married, which makes me wonder if Jenny Cooper is somewhere out there wearing a trucker hat and Lululemon outfit.

Probably not.

The brunette no-longer-hot mom pulls an Amex card from her Chanel shoulder bag and pushes the plastic across the counter, masterfully avoiding potential disruption of her announcement regarding an online course she's taking on manifesting.

My aunt gave me a book for my birthday called *The Secret*, where some lady wrote about how everything she wanted, every single *someday*, came into her life by wishing it would happen. She needed some money, she thought about it, and a check showed up in her mailbox that afternoon.

She called it *the law of attraction.*

Is that the same thing as manifesting?

Because if that's the case, I've been doing a whole lot of manifesting lately, but exactly none of my somedays have materialized. No massively successful music career, no rad wife, no kid to throw a ball with in the yard. And no feeling like I belong, even without a family.

The only somedays that have materialized involve my couch, the Internet, and *Family Feud.*

Maybe I totally fucked up the manifesting formula, and all this time I've been actually trying to manifest *someday I want to be a lukewarm, tepid wuss.*

In which case, I'm living proof that manifesting does indeed work.

Oh, and those not-as-hot moms are both suuuuuuperbusy, but they'll totally catch up over triple-shot extra-dry cappuccinos soon. The blonde one has to run, because she's picking up Blaine from soccer practice. He's obviously the best forward on the club travel team, even though the coach won't say it.

suuuuuuperbusy *(adj)*
a claimed state of false productivity, usually referenced to influence outside perception

I mean, everybody knows.

GET A PUPPY FIRST

The brunette used-to-be hot mom waits for the blonde to be out of earshot before motor-boating her mouth in scoffing disagreement. I see a window and offer her a wry smile.

She probably should've gotten a puppy first.

She glares at me with a raised eyebrow, glossed lips caught somewhere between *who the fuck are you* and *why are you talking*, takes position behind her cart, and parades into the parking lot.

I should've known better. I already lost one semi-friend because of a single unsolicited parenting observation, in this very same Trader Joe's. I'd just grabbed my customary three boxes of granola when I noticed the semi-friend scrutinizing the ingredients on a box of Tasty O's, before disapprovingly shoving the cereal back on the wrong shelf.

Her kid was stuffed into the front seat of the shopping cart, repeatedly crying *McDonald's*, and threateningly wielding a gold trophy with a baseball player on top. I said hello to her and high-fived the kid in between his sobs, congratulating him on the win.

She whispered that his team didn't *actually win*, but everyone in the tournament got a trophy, and he deserved recognition for at least showing up. Especially since he didn't want to play, because he doesn't like the other kids, and got in trouble with the coach last week for pooping behind the dugout.

She'd briefly considered my mating potential many moons ago, after I played a show with one of her favorite artists. We sat at the bar after my set, and within a half-Budweiser, I'd already become well-versed in her *mememe* childhood and the ignorant, blissful vagrancies rooted in her refusal to take responsibility for any living thing, herself included. Well, besides the goldfish she brought home from the State Fair, which died two days later.

mememe *(adj) self-obsessing, with limited awareness of, and no concern for, circumstances outside one's own whims*

We stayed in text-touch, after my reluctance to be unconditionally admiring fatally damaged my spouse-eligibility. She eventually met some selfish prick that never had to take care of anything else either, they boned down, and nine months later woke up to this living, breathing thing wholly dependent on them.

And now she's apparently offended at the mere thought of her 7-year-old eating Tasty-O's with GMOs or gluten or whatever the newest thing is to be scared of, before driving him across state lines to a meaningless baseball tournament, where she and her shotgun-husband can yell at the umpire and take home trophies for 79th place.

All I did was ask why, if the real world doesn't reward barely trying and definitely failing, she'd want to teach her kid other-

59

wise. That approach was setting him up for an entitled lifetime of disappointment, right?

Her eyes widened like I'd shot her first-born in the knee with a pellet gun. She stuttered a non-sensical, shocked response, and stormed away toward the cheese section, never to be texted from again.

I inherited a 7-week-old big brown puppy when my soon-to-be-helicopter-parent-ex-semi-friend could barely take care of her partying self. I taught that dog to wait patiently for her food, and poop where she was supposed to, and to play well with others, and not to whine if she didn't get her way.

Life skills my ex-semi-friend apparently can't teach her kid.

Which is why she'd should've gotten a puppy first.

She would've had to make sacrifices, like coming home early from the rave, apologetically high on pilfered Molly and loving every other Burning Man alum she brushed against, because she had to let the dog out before it shat inside. She would've had to watch something she loved get hurt. And think clearly about what to do next, instead of flying off into crazy-land whenever there was a little blood.

And she may have had to watch that thing she loved die.

But she jumped right into sooooooo-cute-now-I-feel-needed-my-child-is-already-a-star-baby-land, and soon it'll be all of our problem when the spoiled kid devolves into a resource-sucking shitbag living in her basement, on her unlimited data plan, and covered by her health insurance, which I'm probably already paying for thanks to Obama, who seems like he'd be a cool guy to hang out with.

So, yeah. Close the Pinterest page splashed with decorating ideas for the maybe-baby's nursery, spend a couple of hours at the local animal shelter, and do humanity a favor.

Get a puppy first.

SPONSORED

I find a pitch-optional low harmony and sing with Springsteen about how our souls went missing, as we sat listening to the minutes ticking away, wasting time online waiting for life to begin, while it was outside slipping away. I adapt some of the lyrics to my own situation, of course, except the one about how it's a sad man my friend, who's living in his own skin, and can't stand the company.

This road home traces against asphalt that once carried me toward an unknown future, colored with possibility: same road, same unknown future, different hue today.

I stop at the four-way intersection where my Ponch and Jon adventure began and look both ways. My foot is leaving Leia's brake when a heavily branded spandex outfit, perched on a road bike with skinny tires and a million gears, flies past Leia's hood, with a middle finger in the air.

Pointed at me.

I'm not against middle fingers in the air. Last night I had my own bleeding bird pointed at the universe, after a knife sliced between the second and third knuckle.

I've read enough hippie bullshit to understand that whatever goes wrong is my fault, and whatever goes right is thanks to the universe. Sort of like giving God all of the credit and none of the blame.

A concerned neighborhood Secret Santa even gave me a mug last week with *The Universe Knows* etched into the ceramic. If that's the case, the all-knowing, trust-me universe could've just as easily let that blade slide out of the wood block, instead of catching an edge and Freddy-Kruegering my middle finger, which is why I promptly held it to the sky.

A middle finger, immune to traffic and road rules, sent by a shit-bag wearing a stretchy uniform splattered with logos, is surely worse than one coming from somebody like me.

Right?

The sizable baby bump hanging over this guy's waistband suggests he's more likely sponsored by his wallet than any of the brands he's advertising on his outfit. I suppose we have that in common.

I hypothesized that putting Gotcha and Maui and Sons stickers on my surfboard in junior high school would make the cool kids believe those rad companies wanted me to surf for them. I'd belong. I'd matter. I'd be sponsored. Nobody saw me buy the stickers at the surf shop with my allowance, but nobody believed I was sponsored, either.

My Gotcha and Maui and Sons is his Livestrong. This guy probably just wants to matter, too.

Except the cyclist that started Livestrong was exposed as a lying, doping, cheating opportunist, and I wasn't blowing through stop signs on my surfboard and flicking off law-abiding motorists, further proof of the exponential expansion of the douche-factor in urban cyclists. A totally kind, considerate person might buy a road bike, and within a couple of misguided weekends, devolve into a hubrash shitbag who doesn't believe the same set of rules applies to them.

I tailed a gaggle of this same breed of cyclists last week. They were too cool to ride single-file in the designated bike lane, and knew they had strength in numbers, so they took up the entire road.

hubrash *(adj)*
characterized by an arrogant blend of self-important egotism and rude, self-assertive behavior.
See also: hubris; brash

I motored right up onto their giant collective ass until they were a couple of feet from Leia's hood, and laid on her horn. Two shitbags in the back flicked me off at first, but they were outnumbered by the three kids on the sidewalk giving me thumbs up, two guys outside the donut shop raising their arms in triumph, and a little old lady in her Fairmont behind me, who gave me a supportive beep and waved.

I didn't stop honking until I took a right about a half-mile later. By then, I'd morphed into John Cougar Mellencamp rolling down Main Street in the "Hurt So Good" music video, with the hot burlesque-ish dancers on his arms and the whole town agape with admiration and handclaps.

This Livestrong cyclist's middle finger begs for a similar reaction, but if I honked right now, I'd probably freak out the Mexican kid walking his bike in the crosswalk.

They shouldn't be deporting Mexican kids who walk their bikes in the crosswalk.

They should be deporting cyclists who run stop signs with their middle fingers in the air.

THEN

Hard gravel fights rubber, as finer siblings dance behind the wheels and into the mid-morning sun reflection in Leia's rear-view mirror. This is where I find what I've left behind, where I remember what I've forgotten. Sometimes I see who I wanted to be, or the guitar-tuner I forgot to pick up at the music store.

Nobody in the crowd of tens will notice if I'm a little off tomorrow night, so we pull into the garage, and a subdued thud under Leia's front right tire reminds me of what else I forgot: the yearbooks of pressboard and paper strewn across the concrete, bound with threads of *Then*, designed to turn back time.

A strings-heavy keyboard melody spills from the dashboard's tinny front speakers. I crank the volume knob to the left to deaden the intrusion, but the riff continues to build, cymbal swirls intensifying, as I search the stereo and my phone for the external source of the late '80s anthem.

Until an agelessly aged Cher beckons me with a suggestive finger, from my mental Mitsubishi rear-projection cabinet television. She gives me a wink, struts across the Navy ship deck, and mounts one of the big cannons, singing about what she'd do if she could turn back time. Nothing about her looks her age, especially her ensemble, born the sultry night a dominatrix met a stripper. She's clearly already trying to turn back time, no *if* about it.

Which continues to work wonders, in an airbrushed Playboy centerfold way, as she fishnets firmly into the pants of every sailor behind her, my non-sea-faring-self included. A familiar teenage prayer stirs in my loins, to any available God, harkening back to my prepubescent plea that my mom wouldn't walk into the den when this video was on MTV.

Everything about it was hot.

And three decades ago.

fishnet *(v)*
to engage in a futile and obvious attempt to turn back time

Then.

Then should be a grateful ghost, reminding me of loving parents that worked long hours to give me Christmas, AYSO uniforms, college tuition, and themselves in every spare minute. *Then* should be an inspiring ghost, pointing me toward living with the simple joy of pounding on the guitar, with the breathless exhilaration of roughhousing with my grandma's dog, with the entire-body presence of dancing with a dream.

But most of the time, *Then* shows as ghosts of cracked hearts in different shades, spirits I can blame for my silent retreat to the safety of quiet introversion.

Last night I watched a ghost-hunting show where this lady went into a house at midnight, saw dead people and the bad shit that happened *Then*, and reported her findings to the homeowners. She told the freaked-out couple that if they just talk to the ghosts, these spirits of the past will move on.

Maybe I should be talking to mine.

UN-FAIR-Y TALES

The fluorescent garage light lingers between sputter and spark as I set the Trader Joe's bag on Leia's hood and bend down to pick up my junior high yearbook, now half-compressed with a black tire streak cutting the cover.

When's the last time you read what I wrote in there?

What?

It's Jenny, silly.

Jenny?

Jenny Cooper.

Where's your voice coming from?

I'm always around. You know that.

I haven't seen you in years, and I don't see you now.

You don't have to see ghosts. Sometimes you hear them. You've watched enough ghost-hunting shows to know that.

Should I be scared? I mean, are you dead?

You're overthinking this. Wait a minute... is that the clip-on tie from Cotillion? Right there, next to that blue cape on the floor, by the box.

No way! You still got that tie?

I briefly cling to the edges of an awestruck, linguistically challenged black hole, before shifting my wide eyes to the blank chalkboard and stuttering *Uhyeahhistillgotthattie.*

Jenny has blossomed into the most beautiful lily amongst a field of adolescent weeds. Lip-gloss has evolved into lipstick. Her unnecessary training bra has developed into a very necessary real bra. Her hair is gelled on one side, and blown dry on the other, like Molly Ringwald.

And she just chose the desk next to me in world geography class on the first day of school, where the first thing I learn is that Belinda Carlisle is right. Heaven is indeed a place on earth, specifically immediately to my left.

Seventh grade left me short in confidence and stature and everything else that mattered to the cool kids, most of whom are now drinking mini-bottles of vodka before gym class, in these first few days of 8th grade. The only thing more horrifying than actual gym class this week was the idea of gym class last summer.

70

I sat on the toilet this past July, eyes trained downward at a barren wasteland, and promised my eternal devotion to any higher power who would sprout some sort of fuzzy growth in that area. No deity answered, likely because the extent of my recent religiosity had been limited to the one afternoon earlier that month when I'd been Jewish.

Jacob Ross was Jewish, too. We spent Saturday nights at each other's houses, staying up late talking about Magic Johnson's latest double-double and wondering why 4th grade society had to be inescapably harsh. We invited each other to our ill-attended birthday parties, and on the weekends played football and soccer and rode skateboards at the junior high school, where we both were now fighting for relevance.

Jacob Ross was my friend.

He invited me to his bar mitzvah that summer before 8th grade. I wasn't exactly sure what a bar mitzvah was, except that it had to do with being Jewish and getting presents. By the time I walked into the synagogue with a wrapped Star Wars action figure and took the first seat I could find, my conversion to Judaism was already in motion.

The lady to my right shot me a sideways disapproving look as I sat down, which I didn't think I deserved. An older bearded man at the front of the synagogue started reading out of a huge book, but he was speaking in tongues, so I was already confused when I stood up.

Everyone else in my row had risen to their feet and started shuffling toward the procession in the aisle to my left. The guy speaking in tongues said a word that sounded like *Go*, and as the line of robed religious-looking people approached, I swore I felt a nudge from the lady next to me.

So I went.

I started to realize I was Jewish as the procession banked right and the rest of the line began chanting. We passed in front of Jacob and his parents, they looked at me like I'd shot a puppy, and I did my best to look official as *Damnyou* rose from my stomach.

The procession took a left, up some stairs into the front of the synagogue. I took a right, walked all the way to the back, pushed open the door, and started running the second my feet hit the sidewalk. I was trying to escape *Damnyou*, and also afraid that an angry mob of bar-mitzvah police would appear if I looked back, so I kept my head down and legs moving as fast as my slacks would allow, replaying my failed Jewishness with embarrassed shame all the way home.

And this is probably why no God answered my ball-fluff prayer. I lost the agonizing struggle to talk my pubic hair into making an appearance by September, and only a couple of post-gym seconds passed yesterday morning before David Schultz noticed my desert privates. He tested relevant nicknames including *Bald Eagle* and *Cue Ball*, the resultant cacophonous laughter roused *Damnyou*, and I rotated to face the tile shower wall, close my eyes, and surrender to the inevitable claws settling into my heart.

This morning, however, the mildew in the tile grout is whispering the promise of my next class, where I'll be king of the world. Not only is today our first quiz in world geography, which I'll get 100% on, but also, Jenny Cooper and I will be within sneezing range of each other.

And whatever she has, I want.

Did you ever think I might want what you have?

Nope. And I didn't think I'd ever see you again after that last night of Cotillion. We went to different schools, and I figured you'd already dropped out of junior high, married a baron, and were living on a yacht in the south of France.

Didn't quite go down that way, did it? I'm starting to wonder if you live most of your life in that introverted head of your's, where you create these stories that become some fake reality.

I suppose you did transfer to my junior high school that fall, instead of marrying a baron and living on a yacht in the south of France.

Right. Why did you invent a story like that?

Probably to explain to myself why, despite our unforgettable dance at the church assembly hall, you probably wouldn't remember me, much less talk to me. Also, I was shy. I needed an excuse to not talk to you.

You know the real tragedy of these un-fair-y tales?

I don't see a problem, no.

You believe them.

DON'T STOP BELIEVIN'

You should read what I wrote in your yearbook.

I covertly duck into a stall in the boy's bathroom at Rogers Junior High School, because everybody in the quad is screaming at each other to have a bitchin' summer, and this ballpoint pen unveiling demands peace and solitude.

The last day of school is here, which means I'm never going to see Jenny Cooper again, since she's going to the big public high school down the street. As soon as Wilson High put up barbed wire around the perimeter, to either keep something out or something in, my mom told me I'd be enrolling somewhere else. Not there, not with Jenny.

A couple of minutes ago, I stared past her at my world geography dreamland going up in flames, as she wrote definitely more than one line on one of my many blank pages. She handed the yearbook back to me, winked, and turned to David Schultz, like she was signing autographs on the red carpet before entering the Schubert Theatre of adolescence.

And now, I'm closing the boys' bathroom stall door and sitting on the toilet to start my frantic flipping to see what she wrote.

A torn yellow corner of a Pee-Chee folder already bookmarks the page holding the most beautiful missive a girl has ever written to me, maybe ever will, full of hidden meaning and nuance I'll re-interpret and un-interpret and mis-interpret for too many years to come.

Most beautiful, because the words are from Jenny.

Hold on. There's also writing on the little piece of Pee Chee bookmark.

Want to get lunch Saturday? 424-2054.

Saturday?

I usually have bologna on Wonder bread with mayonnaise for lunch on Saturdays, before rearranging the furniture in my bedroom into another new world, where I can live at peace with my Star Wars action figures for the next week. This proposed unfamiliar territory demands trusted guidance, so I ask the carved penis on the back of the stall door for advice.

Lunch? Saturday? Where do I get money for lunch? What should I wear?

And the crucial one.

Is this a date?

There's no way I'm letting my mom answer the question about what to wear, which is why I'm consulting the carved penis. The kid across the alley invited me to dinner last week, and I was nonchalantly excited to have been invited by an older kid to do anything. But when I walked downstairs in my jeans and cool-est-possible *Empire Strikes Back* t-shirt, my mom made me go back to my room and change into a collared Lacoste polo with slacks and a cloth woven belt. I felt super lame waiting in line with my friend and his dad at the fast-food Mexican place.

The carved penis suggests my new Maui and Sons shirt, with my red Stanford sweatshirt tied around my striped Gotcha shorts, and reminds me that I kept the ten-dollar bill my mom gave me for that Mexican dinner, since my friend's dad covered my bean and cheese burrito.

David Schultz's caustic growl resonates from the hallway, sig-naling my nemesis' impending arrival. He barrels into the boys' bathroom with a couple of his minions, and I lift my knees to my chin, hold my breath, and pray they won't notice me in here.

The urgency of their pee-sword war, fought partly at the urinals, but mostly at the floor, demands all available mental resources. Ammunition spent, they leave the battlefield as docile as they arrived, and I finish devising my own weekend attack plan with the carved penis.

We primarily focus on advance battle preparation, since we remain unsure if this is an actual date. Neither of us know shit about girls.

I wake up at dawn the next Saturday, stumble downstairs, and turn on the television. I watch the early static snow, until a picture of an American flag flashes on the screen, and the symphonic national anthem opens programming for the day. Scooby Doo, Mighty Mouse and I discuss strategy one last time before my mom comes downstairs to make eggs she won't eat. She finds all things poultry repulsive, her aversion rooted in the mean chickens that pecked her hands raw on her aunt's farm, the summer before she left for the Masonic home.

But I love scrambled eggs with cheese, and she loves me. After breakfast, I take the dirty dishes into the kitchen, and steal a glance into the den, where my combat campaign will commence. I've stealthily laid some groundwork the evening before, while my parents were upstairs in their bedroom, watching Magnum P.I. on the VCR.

I leave the dishes in the sink, slink into the den to avoid interrogation, and take my position next to the Realistic 91 Clarinette AM/FM turntable and cassette deck combo, holding court next to the our threadbare, faded blue couch. A Heath radio kit my dad put together serves as the throne for the Realistic, set on top of a second-hand coffee table. The nicer furniture is in the living room, where no one ever goes.

My sister's vinyl copy of Journey's *Escape* is already locked and loaded in the Realistic, auditory bullets ready to fire. Arming myself with the Koss Pro 4AA wrap-around headphones, I crank the volume, lift the needle…

And pull the trigger.

I fight strong and deep in the first two tracks of Side A, where I'm just a city boy born and raised in south Detroit, where burning love comes once in a lifetime, over and over and over, until there's no way I'll stop believing, because I'm stone in love.

Battle-weary yet sufficiently victorious, I hit *Stop* on the Realistic, take off the headphones, and explode into the kitchen, where our rotary telephone waits on top of the directory perched in the dinette nook. I frantically dial 424-2054, but hang up as soon as the last 4 spins around into the vacuum of *Damnyou*.

All hundred pounds of my sister are thumping the floor above me to a song cranked on the Radio Shack hifi she got for her 16th birthday. Some guy is telling a girl named Jenny that he got her number and needs to make her his, that he tried to call her before but he lost his nerve.

I haven't yet learned that *serendipity* is a hippie way of saying *coincidence*, but as 867-5309 serendipitously thunders through the house, the singer starts sounding more like me. His 867-5309 is my 424-2054. His lost nerve is mine. His Jenny is, too.

The repeating coda fades into radio static, as the DJ's tenor circles above a majestic piano chord and note interplay. This masterpiece guided me on the battlefield moments ago, but instead of one of the greatest rock voices of all time suggesting that I don't stop believin', Steve Perry whispers from my right shoulder.

Dude, she wants to talk to you.

She gave you her number.

DUDE.

Thirty minutes later, Jenny and I meet at a burger place within walking distance of our houses, where I order food for the first time without an adult around. We wait for our number to be called, pick up the styrofoam cups and mesh plastic baskets lined with wax paper, and sit down across from each other in the cockpit of an X-Wing fighter.

When our greasy fingers touch in a mutual reach for fries, the spaceship dives in a thrilling, breathless drop, until Jenny moves her foot under the table to rest against my shin and the rocket ship banks right, until she reaches across the table with a napkin to wipe stray mustard from my cheek and the X-wing accelerates up into the heavens, on a mission to destroy the Death Star of pubescent hell, manned by David Schultz.

And I live inside every single sweaty special awkward moment, as if this beautiful scene in space and time might never come again.

So I was your first date?

Is that really what it was?

Yeah, silly. You never gave yourself enough credit, you know that?

I asked you out. That was a date. Didn't you ever read what I wrote in your yearbook?

I did.

I do.

Well, the year is over and it's getting too sentimental for me I'm really going to hate leaving and I'm dreading the thought of coming back since you won't be here. I'll never forget you; you mean a lot to me! Take care! Love always

HEAVEN

Murmurs become rumors in these cerebral hallways, where a quiet, honest hint of doubt behind a locked door can fester into a consuming, chaotic infection. I believed Jenny carried the key in the back pocket of her acid-washed Guess jeans, that she could turn the brass knob, push open the wooden slab, and let these small stirrings escape, before they grew into debilitating screams.

Look at your mangled freshman yearbook, torn open right there under the tire. You can see us in that photo, in the middle of the gym floor!

That's because nobody else wanted to slow dance to Bryan Adams.

Your first concert, right?

I can't believe I told you that.

Well, I can't believe you almost didn't ask me to that Homecoming dance.

I assumed you were already gone. You know, fake ID, backstage hangs at U2 concerts, desert raves, high school domination.

You and your stories. Your whole family went to my high school, didn't they?

I think my grandfather was in the second graduating class. And both of my parents, my aunts and uncles, and all our family friends went there. Even my sister, who was a cheerleader and Homecoming queen. Not meant to be for the runt.

Please. Lose the self-deprecation act. I don't blame your mom for finding you a smaller school. You seemed to be a late bloomer, different from the kids I was hanging around with at that bigger school.

Those kids were at my smaller school, too. I tried to make some friends that first week, but most of them had already gravitated toward the popular celestial bodies they'd revolve around for the next four years.

And you hadn't done anything celestial, huh?

You mean like steal liquor from my dad's cabinet, or smoke good weed, or screw Linda under the bleachers?

I figured you wouldn't be screwing anything.

You figured right. The only cool thing I did was meet you at that burger place, which is why I asked you to Homecoming.

That's sweet. I was excited when you called.

83

I was so nervous. We had this new push-button phone in the kitchen, and I didn't have the luxury of the rotary-dial buffer anymore. I hit that last 4, and I was committed.

Me, too. I wore heels!

Jenny opens the door, and my heart drops to the porch. I try to steady my trembling fingers clutched around the corsage I bought earlier that afternoon as Jenny curtsies, offers her hand, and I slip the flowers on her wrist.

My mom and dad are stationed an appropriate number of car lengths away to drive us to Homecoming. I open the rear passenger door for Jenny, pump my fist when I hear her seatbelt click, then run around the trunk with my hands in the air, like I'm in a spaceship approaching Space Mountain's first drop.

I struggle to regain relative composure, while my parents fabricate conversation with Jenny in the spaces I should occupy, indicated by my dad's expectant glances at me in the rear view mirror. They leave us at the Chart House for a pre-dance dinner and either go someplace else or hang out in the car. I don't ask what they're doing, because I have to be totally focused on the situation in front of me. This is my first time being at a fancy restaurant on my own, and I'm with Jenny Cooper. I have to get this right.

We're seated a canyon away from each other at a huge four-top table, where the waiter says his name is Brad, leaves some menus, and disappears.

Forever.

I'm not sure what to do. If he isn't taking our order, does he have a sixth sense telling him what to bring? Am I supposed to ask somebody where he went? Should I raise my eyebrows twice, like Tom Selleck in *Magnum, P.I.*, at the busboy who brought the bread and water?

I excuse myself and head to the bathroom to weigh my options and check my armpits. Earlier that afternoon, my sister had pointed to the yellow, rigid stains under my T-shirt sleeves and convinced my mom that drastic measures needed to be taken before the dance. She bought me a white, flaky, smell-good stick at the drugstore, which I smeared across each progressively unsuccessful wardrobe change, until my mom yelled at me that we had to go.

On my way to the restroom, I see Brad talking to the hot hostess by the front door. I catch his eye and do the Tom Selleck thing, and he lifts his head to me and winks. I figure that's enough communication. He knows.

Armpits checked and culinary future determined, I sit down across from Jenny in the seat too low for the table, fidget with the huge menu, eat all the bread, and drink all the water.

Brad never comes back.

Damnyou does.

Maybe Brad wants to see us squirm, or he thinks that serving a couple of kids is beneath him, or he wants to screw the hostess. But when we don't show up outside the restaurant an hour and a half later, my dad comes in to find us.

He frowns at the menus still on the table, asks who our waiter is, and I point to Brad loitering in the hostess's orbit. My dad charges to the front of the restaurant, grabs the back of Brad's collar, pulls him outside, and starts tearing him a new asshole.

Subdued, sharp tones of profanity seep through the glass entry doors and wash over the entire restaurant. Jenny and I smile at each other until we're distracted by the blur of the manager, running to stop the carnage. My dad tears an even bigger gash out of that guy, knifing him with *kids* and *respect* and *humanity* and *your own child* and *that hostess is half your age*, pierced with a million creatively placed cuss words.

A pause for patriarchal breath allows space for a single clap to break the rapt, engaged silence that's fallen over the Chart House. Another clap sounds, and another, and I look past Jenny to see the older man and his wife applauding at the table next to us. The people next to them start clapping, too, and the people next to them.

My dad nods his head at me, I get up, rush around the table, and pull the chair out for Jenny. We walk through the restaurant to escalating cheers and applause, and I even slap a couple of open palms outstretched for high-fives.

My mom buys us burritos at the fast-food Mexican place down the street, and we eat them in the back seat on the way to the dance. Jenny touches my knee and tells me that a burrito is better than any fancy dinner.

Homecoming is almost over by the time we get there. We walk under the streamers, and I'm so proud to have Jenny on my arm, but before I can gauge the surely awestruck reaction of the entire school and faculty, the first few notes of "Heaven" reverberate off the wooden gym floor.

I love Bryan Adams, but apparently nobody else in my new high school does, because nobody is heading to mid-court. I'm not nobody, though. I'm with Jenny Cooper, which makes me somebody.

I take her wrist, lead her to the center-stripe, and face her, nervously averting my gaze, in shock at my sudden boldness. She reaches across the divide, cradles my head in her hands, and forces me to look straight at her.

Into windows of everything I believed I couldn't be.

Until now.

WEED

A harsh uncertainty flashes across the unfinished drywall, the dying strobe spasming over a disillusioned Gen X-er kneeling next to a tattered box, clutching again in trembling fingers a now wilted, dried corsage. Only two petals remain of what was left on the back seat of his parents' car the night he felt the fresh flowers brush the top of his hand, then fingers on his wrist, fingers on his palm, fingers in his, all the way home.

He gets to his feet with the keys to an X-Wing fighter and leads what used to be out to the middle of the concrete floor, where a small circle shines from the automatic garage door light. He holds his arm up and out at a right angle, in the proper Cotillion position he learned at the church assembly hall, and what used to be pulls his hand around to the small of her back and the spaceship dives in a thrilling, breathless drop, until she interlocks her arms through his and the rocket ship banks right, until she rests her head on his shoulder, and the X-wing accelerates up into the heavens, where David Schultz can't even breathe, all while Bryan Adams sings about our younger years when we were young and wild and free.

And he lives inside every single sweaty special awkward moment, as if this beautiful scene in space and time might never come again.

The automatic garage door light shuts off and I gently tuck the fragile few remaining petals into the safer confines of my jeans pocket, wondering if whatever she saw in me disappeared with the rest of the corsage.

Heart. That's what I saw.

Heart? Heart didn't matter on the playground or in high school. The cool kids didn't care about heart, and the rest of the world seemed to care about the cool kids.

I sort of became one of them.

I heard you started hanging out with friends who had older brothers buying you beer and selling you weed. And I heard about the tattoos you were getting and the parties you were throwing. You moved into a world I knew nothing about.

It's not like I didn't want to invite you to those parties. I didn't think you'd be into that scene.

You wouldn't have wanted me there, not after the Weed Incident.

The Weed Incident?

I never told you about that?

Uh, no.

I slip in uninvited through the back door of a popular girl's party, camouflaging my jeans and gray t-shirt against the dark-stained kitchen cabinetry. A few months have passed since Homecoming, and I haven't made in-roads with the cool kids, but I'm hoping I'll be tolerated here.

I flop around her house like a pimply fish out of action-figure water, until a B-list kid gives me unsolicited advice to eat a pot brownie for the oldest, dumbest reason in the growing-up playbook: everyone else is doing it.

I can't tell if I feel anything, given the uncharted waters I'm already navigating. I do get hungry, so when I walk past the pile of brownies on my way to the bathroom, I eat two more.

Within twenty minutes I'm propped up in the corner of the living room, staring straight ahead, with my hands in my crotch and unable to move or talk, even when the popular girl asks me if I need some water.

All I can think is how this will be the last time I'll eat anything with weed in it.

I should've been thinking this will be the last time I'll try to be like everyone else.

What a fucking mistake that is.

BEN

I wish I knew that back then. David Schultz and I both were riding the everyone-is-doing-it train in high school.

Whatever happened to him?

He got busted freshman year for stealing mini-bottles of vodka from the corner grocery store. His mom and step-dad fought all the way through high school to keep him out of the juvenile detention system, and last I heard, he'd been arrested for something bigger that no one would talk about.

I never did have the balls to tell David Schultz to fuck off, but apparently the universe took care of that.

Yeah, it did. What did the rest of high school look like for you?

Same not asking the prettiest girl out, not paddling for the best wave, staying in between the lines, playing by the rules. And making sure I had my mom's approval.

That doesn't sound like Sixteen Candles.

No, more like a post-pubescent *Graduate* without Mrs. Robinson. Or her daughter. I guess I couldn't find solid footing on social ground.

How come?

Most of the kids moved past weed and onto harder stuff, which sort of changed them into different people and made me feel like I wasn't good enough, because they didn't really care about hanging out with me. They cared about hanging out with their other, higher selves, and possibly me as collateral necessity.

You shouldn't have taken it so personally.

How could I not, when I was facilitating them getting high in my vacationing parents' living room, cleaning up the ensuing apocalyptic destruction and taking them to the abortion clinic a couple of months later.

I wouldn't have done that to you. And you didn't have to do that for them, either.

I know. I'm still cleaning up messes, only now they're mostly left on the side of the trail by shitbags. I just hoped that enabling those cool kids would help me not feel as left out. Ben took the other road, and I didn't want to go there.

Ben?

Where's my senior yearbook?

Is that it, next to the water heater?

Yeah. Here, look.

Why is there a full-page photo of you?

Each senior had their own yearbook page, where we put inspirational quotes and photos of ourselves looking like bad-asses, or contemplative, or attractive, or whatever we were hoping to project into the waiting, skeptical world.

'You can't always get what you want, but if you try sometimes, you might find you get what you need.' Is this what you wanted me to see?

No. Look at the opposite page.

There's only a name, a grainy photo, and a couple of dates.

197▓ – 198▓

I'm waiting outside Ben's house, in the passenger seat of Grayson Boyd's car. He's honked the horn in brief questioning beeps for about a minute, but Ben's not coming out for carpool.

A motorcycle cop stops next to us, motioning Grayson to drive away. Emergency lights flash across the vinyl interior, and as we turn right at the corner, I see two paramedics bust through the ambulance doors and rush into the house.

I'm drawing surfboards in the margins of my textbook when Mr. Oswald's Ottoman Empire lecture is interrupted by a knock on the classroom door. And this is how I learn that Ben won't be coming out for carpool ever again, because in the half-light before dawn, he shot himself in his mom's bathroom.

Administrators bring guidance counselors to school that day, and everybody tells each other they're going to miss him. The cool kids mope around with too-late confessions of what a good person he was, and the popular girls, who didn't give a fuck about Ben when he was alive, set up a memorial in front of his locker.

People probably wouldn't kill themselves as often if we treated them like they'd just died, while they were still here.

I just noticed we called him by his middle name. We were friends, and I didn't even know that.

You never thought about killing yourself, did you?

Not really, but I wrote my very first song right before Ben died, called "Sanctuary," about a magical place behind the mountains and beneath the ocean where I could disappear to. I think a lot of people wonder how the world would react if they weren't around.

I'm one of them. You do know that most of those cool kids probably felt left out at some point, too, which is why they were separating into cliques and getting high in the first place. That's what happened to me.

How is that possible? You seemed to be the epitome of beautiful and popular.

You only saw me at school. A different world was waiting at home.

What kind of world?

I'm not here to talk about me. Let's just say we're all carrying a burden, and looking for ways to lighten the load.

But...

No.

Jenny...

I said No. And now I'm changing the subject. What's this little felt pouch next to the Batman cape?

Don't take that out.

Is this a fraternity pledge pin?

Maybe.

95

You made a promise to a fraternity?

No, I made a promise to you. Remember?

THE PROMISE

A bright-sky Tuesday shines on our street-side aluminum mailbox, a beacon of new beginnings. I've rushed home during lunch break because today is the day, today is when everything changes, today is when I show the world that I belong, today is the day I pull out 8 thin, single-page envelopes and set them gently on the center console, next to the disbelief and sadness that accompany me back to baseball practice.

I've dedicated my entire high school experience to getting into the right college, because receiving a thick package in the mailbox from an elite school will dwarf the lack of acceptance I feel everywhere else. And all my life, my achievement in the classroom has been my own special life raft, keeping me above water and safe from drowning in the sea of perceived peer injustices.

The floatation device just started losing air fast, and I'm not sure I can swim.

Grayson knocks on a bathroom stall in the boy's locker room later that afternoon, where I've hidden myself away so only the toilet can witness *Damnyou* pouring frustrated, unaccepted, not-good-enough water out of my eyes. He asks me what's wrong, and when I slide the rejection letters under the stall door, he kicks the metal latch open with his cleat, pulls me off the toilet, puts his arm around me, and says *Fuck 'em* over and over as we walk up to the field.

I drive home after practice and the first song that comes on the radio is by Tom Petty, with a chorus about how even the losers get lucky sometimes.

I hope he's right.

The 9th letter comes the next day, but this is a thickish package from a huge state university a handful of freeway miles away. I accept their accepting me and enroll, with plans to transfer when I prove I'm good enough.

Two weeks into my freshman year, I'm hearing stories around campus about everyone else's soon-to-be-legendary Dirk Digler exploits. Driven to the brink of sexual desperation and forced to examine all available de-virginizing options, I make the ill-advised decision to join a fraternity.

I'd rather be the master of my own little world, even without the action figures, so this move is strictly lower-half inspired. I have the inane expectation, largely based on an adolescent screening of *Animal House*, that my virginity will be no match for the aphrodisiac of a hundred not-quite-men doing keg-stands and pounding beers at Thursday night mixers. No sufficiently attractive and willing dame could resist such temptation.

Toward the end of rush week, a well-meaning, all-American-boy-next-door president pokes a pledge pin through my chest pocket and presses a felt pouch into my hand, so I'll be able to protect this symbol of worthiness long after I'm a real brother. My days of purity are surely numbered.

I spend a total of two nights at the fraternity house, where the hallway soundtrack of drunken heaves steals whatever sporadic sleep I can muster, and the remainder of my freshman year on my sister's couch. A fortunate educational twist of fate has landed her in a graduate program at the same school, and her freezer stocked with Oreo Chocolate Cookie Dough ice cream sends me home for the summer about 15 pounds heavier and a committed virgin, convinced that I'm never going to get laid. Ever.

I'm picking up a gift from the neighbor's dog in my parents' front yard one July afternoon when a topless Jeep rolls into the driveway. The manual transmission fights the driveway grade, until a girl with long blonde hair blowing across her Ray-Bans engages the emergency brake, kills the engine, and smiles.

Almost five years have passed since we've seen each other. Jenny says she was nowhere near my neighborhood, which seems like a good reason to stop by, and also sounds like a line I've already heard in a movie.

My heart says she's the same Jenny I remember from the Homecoming dance, but my eyes tell me she's not. Even behind her aviators, she looks weathered and tired. Peeking out from her waistline is a tattoo of a dolphin, surrounded by stars with the word *Dreamer*.

She already has a past.

Doesn't matter.

To me, she will forever be beautiful.

She's working as a pastry chef at a restaurant in our hometown, and I visit her whenever I can break away from my mom's disapproving glare. A kiss behind the delivery bay leads to a futon in her studio apartment, leads to clumsy fingers fumbling with a bra strap, leads to jeans piled on the floor, leads to her ring finger tracing my sweaty spine.

If my most beautiful moments until now seemed like a thrilling ride in an X-Wing fighter, this is a floating, shared breath of time suspended in space, circling light years above a beautiful blue sphere, a more perfect world than I ever will see again.

I knew.

Well, I'd hope you knew. One pump and done.

No, I mean I could tell what it meant to you. And I saw something else in you that I'd already lost. That's why I asked you to never do anything to your body. No tattoos, no piercings, no nothing.

You could've asked me to pull out my own toenails and I would've said ok.

But you made a promise.

Which I almost broke a few years down the road.

You did?

I walked into a tattoo parlor a couple of doors down from the Tractor Tavern in Seattle, with foggy plans to get my own barbed-wire-and-feather ink eruption around my pasty bicep.

Tell me you didn't go through with it.

Well, I was feeling strong after playing an opening set of songs at the Tractor, before a local hero's headlining show.

Pull up your sleeve. Right now.

Don't worry. I didn't break the promise. Haven't yet. Never will.

Sometimes I wonder what would have happened if I hadn't broken mine to you... all those pledges of my eternal love.

Me, too.

I guess we do the best we can with what we have at the time, you know?

Sometimes we do. But I think sometimes we don't.

What's with the letters in this box, bundled up with a rubber band? You kept all of these?

Yeah. You sent one every week, about how you wanted to scream your love for me to the world, about how you couldn't wait to make me happy, about how you couldn't imagine your life without me. Nobody's ever written anything like that to me, so I kept them.

This is weird. The handwriting looks different in some of these letters, almost like another person was holding the pen.

I figured you were writing late at night, when you were tired. Or you were on the bus to work. Anything other than what the real reason ended up being.

I remember now. I don't know what to say. Except I'm sorry.

I come home from Statistics 40 on Halloween afternoon of my sophomore year to a blinking *1* on the answering machine. Jenny's voice sounds hurried and uncertain, like she doesn't know what to say, but by the third listen I can decipher that she doesn't want to see me anymore and I have to leave her alone.

I call her right away and talk to her answering machine, which I keep doing once a week, all the way through Christmas break and into the next semester. And while the rest of college is having the time of their lives on their parents' dime, *Damnyou* and I sit on the futon, waiting for a call.

Almost a decade passes, until one wet Seattle morning, a thousand miles from that futon, a million steps forward and two million back, the telephone rings.

FAMILY FEUD

Tammy! Tell me about yourself. Says here you're the mother of 5?

The most famous mustache on the rehashed game-show circuit is introducing family members in the living room, his man-ufactured enthusiasm leaking under the door to the garage. I miss the original host, Richard Dawson, whose kissing-every-fe-male-guest habit teetered between creepy and endearing, de-pending on the victim.

I'm starting to call the Family Feud family members by the in-side-joke nicknames I've made up for them. I'm also making up stories about where they live and what they fight about and what's in their fridge. And sometimes I plan my night around watching Family Feud, as if the new mustached-host will be a late-night savior from another suckout day.

Top five answers on the board, we asked 100 people why you aren't not happy, but aren't happy, either.

suckout *(adj) characterized by the slow drain of inspiration and meaning*

There's no such thing as happy.

103

Suuurrrrrvvey says X. First strike on the board.

I don't have what I need to be happy.

XX. Second strike.

Screw this stupid question.

XXX.

Whatever. Giving a shit about what 100 surveyed people think hasn't been working out, anyway.

HIT ME UP

I rescue the Trader Joe's bag from Leia's hood and shoulder-push the door open into the living room. Changing the channel to a football game, I leave the remote on the coffee table next to an invitation to my high school reunion, which is amongst the two pieces of mail I've received this month actually addressed to me.

I also got one perfect-family-photo-our-life-is-suuuuuperbusy-and-rad Christmas card. This particular old-school version of Instagram featured an update on the back, including under-12 youth baseball tournament wins and a trip to Spain, but mysteriously left out Jack's affair and Hailey's rehab.

I'm not going. To the high school reunion, that is. Things aren't exactly awesome at the moment, and I don't need to stand in a circle with a drink at the proper just-below-rib-cage height, so I can make shit up with people who didn't invite me to their parties 25 years ago.

And still don't.

Christmas decorations were starting to grace the neighborhood when I reached out to a guy who'd presided over a cool clique in high school. From the cut of his hip suit and relaxed smile in the glossy alumni magazine photos, his reign continued into adulthood.

The article about him ended with a *Hey y'all, hit me up on Facebook!*

So, I did. I hit him up on Facebook, because I wanted to believe that the popular kids from high school had changed. Or, maybe I retreated too far into my books and songs as a teenager, settling for the safety of the known at the expense of my real life somewhere out there. Maybe I needed to change then, and I need to change now.

I composed a long-time-no-talk message about how I wanted to reconnect, feeling my own douche-factor rise as I pecked out *r-e-c-o-n-n-e-c-t*. An unsettling dirtiness intensified with each phrase, crafted to mend a fence this guy didn't even know existed, let alone was broken.

He replied with a couple of sentences about being married and having kids and living in LA and loving life, which I'd already gleaned from his perfect Facebook profile with a pinned post announcing his family's annual Christmas party. I wrote back that I didn't have a wife or kids, but we should get together sometime, possibly at his Christmas party, if he let me know where to go.

He didn't respond. I waited a couple of weeks before following up. No reply. I tried again last week. Nothing. And yesterday.

Nopification.

And here I am now, checking my phone again for a little red sign to tell me I'm ok.

I wonder what Luke Skywalker's heroic journey would've looked like with an iPhone attached to his hip, instead of a light saber. He could've still pulled out an electromagnetic piece of radiating metal and hit a button to make it glow, but instead of fighting evil and darkness, he would've been searching a screen for assurance that he wasn't as lonely as he felt.

That's what I get for putting myself out there. At least I learned that *Hit me up* means *I don't really give a fuck*.

That guy will probably be at the high school reunion, well-dressed and well-wifed and well-off, standing in a circle with a drink at the proper just-below-rib-cage height, making shit up with people that he invited to his parties 25 years ago.

And still does.

Not much has changed since high school.

For either of us.

REFUCK

The pantry door grunts in protest, tattered remnants of its rubber sweep begrudgingly clinging to the hardwood floor. The heel of my hand brushes against a warmfuzzy as I reach for the light switch, in my quest to stash the cereal and pasta I won't be taking on the plane.

Mrs. Bryant would sometimes give me a warmfuzzy for being nice in kindergarten, which I'd pet under my desk, pretending the soft, hide-backed fur was a miniature dog. This warmfuzzy, however, was alive until very recently, but now dangles in an apparent suicide from the shelf above the granola bars.

I stumbled into the kitchen pre-coffee a Sunday ago and thought I saw a mouse scoot under the pantry door. I couldn't tell in my dawn haze if he was real, or even a he, but over the next few days, a very real rodent with a little notch in his ear charted several courses across the living room. A navigational miscue landed him on the couch cushion closest to the Christmas tree, so I named him Christmas.

Giving him a name led to an irrational level of concern for his well-being. The next morning, I heard a faint, tiny scratching in the garage and rescued him from open-air drowning in an upright plastic Home Depot bucket. I coaxed him into the bushes behind the house, where I left mozzarella cheese from a leftover pizza to sustain him.

Later that night, I discovered mouse turds in my pasta, and by the next morning, Christmas had shat on almost every edible thing in the pantry. I salvaged what I could into a Tupperware bin, which he chomped through that afternoon, leaving both turds and little pieces of plastic everywhere, including inside my last box of Trader Joe's macaroni and cheese.

I reluctantly searched, and more reluctantly found, an old-school mousetrap on the highest shelf in the garage, next to some unopened car wax. I didn't want to kill Christmas, but I was running out of options.

I set the trap and went to bed with unnecessary conflicted emotions, because by the time I woke up, Christmas had devoured the slathered peanut butter, without tripping the lever to unleash the guillotine. Wracked with attempted murder guilt, I installed a heavy-duty rubber sweep under the pantry door to block his entry, which he chewed through before squeezing into the duct-taped Tupperware bin, and culling one of my last granola bars.

The universe had clearly spoken. We were meant to be together, and over a shared piece of bagel this morning, I invited Christmas to spend his life with me.

So I'm not only horrified at the sight of Christmas blood-splatters on the shelf, I'm also experiencing profound guilt for not discarding the mousetrap after my pledge of unity. And I'm mad, because he'd already cleaned the mousetrap dry, so he had no reason to even be near it. I'd given him every chance to avoid this fate, from the bucket rescue, to leaving him outside with food, to restricting access via the Tupperware bin, and finally the door sweep.

I know, he was a mouse and didn't have a brain like I do, so he couldn't reason like me, which is why he refucked himself to death. But being human doesn't inherently make me smarter than a mouse. Lots of people do the same thing over and over, trying to get what they think they want, until they overdose on their yacht after their prostitute shoots them up in Santa Cruz, or get busted for faking their own hate crime in Chicago.

refuck *(v)*
to repeatedly engage in eventually self-destructive behavior

And it's usually not what they want, it's what the Joneses and *People* and Instagram and Facebook and the Kardashians tell them they want.

Those people are a lot like Christmas.

Wait. Maybe they're not.

He wasn't trying to get what he thought he wanted.

He was trying to get what he actually needed.

Now I really feel bad.

110

I climb on the dresser in the bedroom closet to reach the top shelf, and lift the Cole Haans from their original shoebox. Thin black threads bind stiff saddle-brown leather, barely creased from their single moment of service 25 years ago. Someone might discover these shoes in the gently used bin at the Goodwill store and wear them proudly, like I did to a Homecoming dance, which is why I can't bring myself to donate them.

I take the coffin into the kitchen, pry the metal from the spine of the mouse, and shake the trap until he falls into the shoebox. Wrapping the lid with duct tape, I head into the garage, grab a shovel, open the overhead door, and walk down the driveway, until I find a soft patch under the biggest pepper tree.

And I bury Christmas.

DEICISION

This second-floor living room window faces west, over a one-way residential street canopied with high-voltage wires. If I jumped from here, I could swing on the electric vines into my neighbor's yard. He immigrated from Venezuela with his stunning, kind wife before their country collapsed, and now their weekly house parties last into the early morning hours, constant celebrations born in joy, relief, and escape.

They graciously invited me over when I first moved here, but I pulled an Irish goodbye 15 minutes into reliving the popular high school girl's party. Their beautiful ex-pat South American friends were exotic, which left me BlairWitching in the corner again, and this time I couldn't blame the weed.

BlairWitching (v) *to take a defeated, defenseless position, in anticipation of an undesired fate See also: final scene of the Blair Witch Project*

Afternoon sunlight hasn't yet penetrated the streaks left by the wet nose of a lost partner, memories I can't bring myself to wipe away. I have some time before I need to shower, pack, and rehearse a couple of songs, so I sink into the couch to watch the end of the football game on TV, which has gone to triple overtime while I've been burying Christmas.

I boost the volume on the TV to better bring myself back to the present moment. Not my present moment, of course. This one belongs to a team that hasn't won a playoff game in three decades. I watch them battle their division rival, and upon their sudden-death field-goal win, offer my own triumphant outburst to the TV. I love this underdog, dark horse shit.

Until some impossibly good-looking gajillionaire quarterback opens his mouth in the post-game interview. He thanks God for choosing to give his team the win, and then he says *I could feel His hand on mine, guiding me to victory.*

I wonder if this guy has any idea how cruel his words are to the rest of the world that God *isn't* choosing. Because if this quarterback really thinks that God chose him to win, that means God didn't choose the other guy. I'm not positive about this, because no one knows anything about God. They believe, which is fine, but not the same as knowing.

And I'm not saying I know for a fact that there's not some higher power out there. I'm just not saying that I know for a fact that there definitely is some higher power out there.

But if there is, I'm pretty sure God wasn't watching this game with his girl on some cloud-couch, telling her who's side He was going to take.

You know, I like that guy better on that other team with the wings on their helmets. I already gave him a hot wife, but I'm going to give him the win, too. And I'm going to make sure that other quarterback takes one in the nuts and can't play for a while. Fuck that other team.

I don't know if this quarterback has been watching the news lately, but if God takes sides like that, He's doing a shitty job in his deicision-making. He chooses America, but changes his mind and flies airplanes into her heart. He chooses Islamic extremists to fight for his will, but changes his mind and chooses moderate Christians to fight the Islamic extremists.

deicision *(n)*
the display of preferential treatment by a deity or other higher power

And then He chooses this guy and his football team.

Is that what kind of God we want to believe in?

That quarterback's wife *is* hot, though.

God got that right.

JIM

I loosen the metal clasp of my belt, detonating a denim building into slow collapse on the bathroom floor, and step into the scalding shower. I get what I consider my best thinking done in here, but I'm starting to reconsider what I consider, so I quickly engage in a cursory wash of my dark parts, before closing the valve.

Steam has already rendered the mirror an index-finger canvas, where I trace a question mark, and by the time I take a towel from the rack, the trail has already refilled with condensation. I don't want to open the window, for fear of losing the swaddling humidity, so the mist sits like a stubborn toddler, even after a hand-swipe across the glass.

As I stare at the tiny droplets where my face should be, struggling to hear the post-game show's distant blathering from the living room, a faint, meek query slips out of the mirror.

Remember me?

No, I don't.

Come on. You remember. My office shared a wall with your interior cubicle at that financial services company. I think it was your first job out of college.

Jim?

You DO remember.

Why are you here?

To hold up a mirror, son.

A mirror?

Yeah. You and me, we're the same.

How? You were practically AARP-enrolled when we met. Seemed like you'd spent your whole career clinging to a middle management rung with those tired, brittle fingers.

That's descriptive. And painful. I didn't think it was that obvious. How could you tell?

Sorry. Sometimes we'd order from the food truck parked on Federal Street, eat by the fountain, and watch people pass by in a hurry. You'd wonder how much money they were spending on take-out lunches and coffees, when they could be saving for some kind of dream someday.

I remember. Someday.

Well, we'd talk, so I knew.

But we talked mostly about you, right? We never talked that much about me.

No, because I didn't ask about your personal life. I figured you'd tell me if you wanted to, and besides, I was only a 21-year-old kid.

But once in a while, I'd steal a glance as you stared at a pretty girl walking by, and there'd be a far-away, wistful, sad look in your eyes, like you were remembering a beautiful moment that never happened.

That's where most of my dreams lived. In the past, in a beautiful memory I had to make up. And that's why I'd take you to lunch and ask about what you wanted out of life.

I didn't want you to become me.

I'm sitting in my cubicle on a frigid February Monday morning, pretending to be busy, while staring at a list of dog names I've pinned to the felt wall behind my computer monitor. My officemate is daydreaming, too, through the small window next to his desk. Jim invariably engages in this ritual the morning after.

He likes to ski and has never married, so he signs up for weekend singles trips to the mountains outside of Boston, looking for somebody who will love him, under the guise of finding some pretty good snow. Whenever I pull his attention away from the window the morning after with a hopeful interrogation, he shakes his head with the same reply about how the right one has always been hard for him to find.

But the snow? The snow is always pretty good.

Jim gathers his overcoat and wallet, takes a fresh-breath hit from a travel-sized tube of toothpaste in his desk drawer, and heads toward the elevator. Sometimes we have lunch together in the break room or outside if the weather cooperates, but on these mornings-after, Jim goes to Burger King by himself and brings an early lunch of a Whopper, medium fries, and a medium Coke back to his desk.

He asked about my dreams last fall by the fountain, while we ate tacos from the food truck and watched the girls walk by in office dresses and sneakers, with the heels of their work shoes poking out of their handbags. I told him that someday I wanted to be a songwriter, which is another way to talk to people without having to talk to them, and he said I came to the right coast, since Bruce Springsteen lives right down the turnpike in New Jersey.

I'd love to summer with Springsteen, but I wanted to live somewhere out west, with real trees, instead of in this concrete forest.

That night after work, I took the subway to the Kenmore Square stop and trudged to my studio apartment above Boston Beer Works, where I medicated my loneliness with pasta and Cops reruns, whose derelict stars helped me rationalize my sanitized life. I washed my dishes by hand and watched the dirty water circle the drain, assigned the same fate to my early twenties, and went to bed, replaying those moments I loved as a kid playing with my grandma's little poodle.

I told myself a dog would fill the space.

I didn't tell anybody else about that, except Jim, the next time we had lunch by the fountain.

And now, he reminds me of my dreams, every Monday morning after a ski trip, amidst limp fries from Burger King. He just sat back down at his desk with the grease-spotted paper bag, and any minute now he'll start dipping one fry at a time in ketchup, between bites, proclaiming *Trees and a dog.*

Motherfucker. Mother fucking fucker.

Whoa. Not the usual reminder. Rough weekend?

Just people. Fucking people. How hard is it to have a little respect for each other? Is it that difficult to not be a self-absorbed asshole?

You said yourself that people fall into two groups. They either get it, or they don't. Self-absorbed assholes don't get it, right?

That's the fucking truth. Thank God for Frasier.

Huh?

All I'm living for is tomorrow night's episode of Frasier on TV, especially when I come in to work Monday morning after one of these ski trips.

Pretty good snow isn't cutting it anymore?

Never has. Neither has this job. I've busted my ass my whole life, and all I have to show for it is this shitty office with a little window, a one-bedroom condo in the suburbs, and ski trips to remind me of how lonesome I am.

Come on man, is it that bad? You're alive.

Am I?

What's that supposed to mean?

I'm sort of here, living, but not really. It's like I stopped halfway to someday.

Halfway to someday?

You take the T into work every morning, right?

Yeah.

Imagine getting on some subway train that carries you in a straight, safe, predictable line of stops. More and more passengers pile in. But you stay standing, ready to get off, in hopes that your sign for Someday will be around the next bend, if you hang on to that aluminum mini-stripper pole long enough.

And you're saying that someday never came.

More like the subway just stopped halfway. Maybe someday would've come if I'd been on a different line. Better yet, I should've just driven myself. I might've stalled out, but at least I'd be driving. Know what I mean?

You're making me rethink my morning commute, Jim.

Well, I lived for someday, you know? Like someday I'd walk off the subway and into the arms of a loving partner and a kid to buy Christmas presents for. And proof that I made a contribution to the world, that I mattered.

But instead I'm crammed in here, can't move, can't get out, and can't feel anything, except these people pushing against me. All I can do is bitch about them to myself. At least getting pissed gives me something else to feel.

So, like I said. Thank God for Frasier.

The next morning, I wake up to Bruce Springsteen singing a song called "Trapped" on my alarm clock radio. He promises that someday he's going to see beyond these walls in front of him, but right now he's trapped.

And by the time the sax solo hits, I can see beyond the walls in front of me. Beyond the felt walls of my cubicle, beyond the concrete walls of this city, beyond the walls I've built around my heart to keep *Damnyou* in check.

I can see trees.

And I can hear the soft pleas of a puppy.

After lunch that day, I walk into my understanding boss's office to give notice. Jim winks as I turn the corner back into my cubicle, waving a hidden thumbs-up behind his desk. I don't even have to tell him that I'm getting off the subway while I can, that I'm driving the rest of the way. He knows.

He follows me to the elevator two weeks later, shakes my hand when the doors ding open, and says *Trees and a dog*. I back into the elevator, facing his small smile and slightly raised hand.

I nod and raise mine, but more in oath than answer.

In oath that I won't let him down.

I'll secure some sort of foothold on the slippery rock face of an impossible dream.

I'll find trees.

And a dog.

Springsteen's "Trapped" opens those exiting elevator doors onto Federal Street, but another song pulls me back across the country to the Pacific Northwest, where a soul-heavy, growling voice has married a gritty guitar riff. The newlyweds wrap themselves around my throat, and the chorus punches through my dashboard speakers, with a message about being 'Alive,' but somehow not.

I'm going where that song lives.

I answer an advertisement in Seattle's local music weekly *The Rocket* for much-needed singing lessons, arrive early at a waterfront house on Alki Beach in West Seattle, and wait in the living room for the eccentric, wet-lipped teacher called Maestro to emerge with a cane, from the hidden bedroom chamber. Black and white photos above the piano of Layne Staley, Chris Cornell, Geoff Tate, Ann Wilson, and other legendary voices are signed with words of gratitude, and I ask Maestro if he taught all of these singers.

He says yes, yes he did, and he thinks a dear boy named Eddie Vedder, too, but he can't be sure, because he teaches many youngsters and he's getting older now.

Maestro records the lesson for me on a cassette tape, which features bombs of life wisdom dropped amongst obstacles blocking the path toward my true voice. He stresses to not sing beautifully, emulate anyone else, or deliver anything other than what is mine.

I take lessons from him every other week for a year, while I work a temp job in Pioneer Square, before tentatively recruiting a band through ads in *The Rocket*. Months of rehearsals in my drummer's moldy basement lead to my first show at the Off-Ramp, where I stand on the same stage that Pearl Jam stood on during their own first show. A DJ will crown us the new breed of Seattle band, *The Rocket* will call me a cross between Eddie Vedder and Bruce Springsteen, and I'll hear a song from my debut EP on the FM dial, right after Springsteen's "Thunder Road."

I meet her at the park, about a block from the house I'm renting in Seattle's Queen Anne neighborhood. She's walking her dog along the chainlink separating the asphalt and grass, where I'm playing with the Labrador I picked up on my way to the Pacific Northwest.

Trees and a dog. Like I promised Jim.

An enthusiastic throw lands the ball at her dog's feet on the other side of the fence, and a couple of hours later we're tangled in my double bed. Over the next year she'll listen to the birth of my songs, come to all of my shows, write me cards of encouragement, and have Easter Brunch with my visiting parents, until Sheryl Crow comes to Seattle for an afternoon outdoor summer concert series.

She knows Sheryl Crow's drummer from some past life, and invites him to dinner with us at her house after the show. She's already told me she needs space, because she can't find the magic anymore, and after the dishes are put away, I can sense her expectation of my impending departure. I leave the two of them in the living room and head to my truck, looking back in time to see her pull the shades slowly down in the bedroom we shared.

Over the next few seasons, other shades are slowly pulled down around me, by a hand I never do see. Grunge's hangover lingers over the exodus of major record labels that came to town on the bandwagon. The crowds at my shows get thinner, as band members move on to other, newly promising towns, and the blanket of Northwest gray settles thicker on my hopes that someday I'll be summering with Bruce Springsteen.

The inaugural generation of Internet monsters spread their tendrils of gentrification into the clubs, bars, and apartments, forcing musicians to the outskirts in search of affordable housing. *The Rocket*, Maestro, and Off-Ramp see their shades pulled slowly down, and soon Layne Staley, Chris Cornell, and Kurt Cobain will join Andrew Wood and watch from atop gravestones as the city they knew, and everything else born in the real dirt of living, disappears into the lamented lore of what used to be.

I write fewer songs, record fewer albums, and play fewer shows, until a brutal blindside haymaker knocks me out of town. I'm sealing packing boxes with tape when a local TV show eulogizes another closed club, this one bought by a hotel developer: the venue where Pearl Jam filmed their video for "Alive."

The song that brought me here.

She's there, during Mike McCready's solo toward the end of the song, her lithe body filling the frame between scenes of stage-diving fans. She's dancing, joyful.

Alive.

In moving pictures, beckoning me toward a dream, 5 years before I'd meet her at the park down the street from my house: the girl who pulled the shade slowly down in the bedroom we shared, the beginning of the end of *Trees and a dog*.

You didn't have to put all that weight in hands capable of pulling the shades slowly down, you know. You have your own hands.

Well, Jim, I thought I might marry that girl someday.

Didn't you remember anything I told you about living for someday?

Yeah, but all these other messages creep in, from TV, radio, the Internet. They make selling today to buy someday seem like a good deal.

And what does someday look like now?

A lot like high school, where a few people decide what's cool and don't have to play by the same rules as everyone else. They marry each other, have babies, give each other killer opportunities, and build these exclusive, smiling, beautiful lives.

At least that's what it looks like on Facebook and Instagram.

Someday *is a dangerous word. You dream about someday, and before you know it, you're complaining about the self-absorbed assholes at your soul-crushing middle-management job.*

Or the self-absorbed assholes on their phones in nature preserves.

Or eating one fry at a time alone at your desk every Monday.

Or soggy fish tacos by yourself in a strip mall parking lot.

Thanking God for Frasier.

And *Family Feud.*

Hopefully it's not too late before you realize your life isn't about manifesting something someday.

It's about living right now.

And right now, you're me.

THE ONE THAT GOT AWAY

Suspended particles of us dance through the stale hallway air, signaling the sun's mid-day journey across a sky-scape cut by the contrails of leaving. Leaving for a better place, for a better man, for a better job. Leaving for a worse place, a worse man, a worse job. Hard to know which at the time.

Dust catching light, or light catching dust.

I walk into the living room, towel around my waist, while I wait for the steam to clear in the bathroom. I should probably run through a couple of songs, if only to feel the guitar's neck in my hands, before I pack her into my gig bag. These days, I don't even remember that I can write or play music, unless I have to rehearse for a show. My guitars hang there on the living room wall, like gravestones of dreams gone by.

I'm not sure why. Maybe the job stole the love. Used to be, I'd write and play to get out whatever was in here, which is probably starting to rot, after not seeing light for so long. But used to be's don't count anymore, they just lay on the floor until we sweep them away. Neil Diamond was right.

I take my Gibson B25 off the wall and collapse into the couch cushions, trying to remember an old Steve Earle song called "Someday" that I might play tomorrow night in honor of Jim. Mr. Earle's got a Chevy, too, except she's a '67, low and sleek and black, and someday he's gonna put her on that interstate and never look back.

The echo of a sensuous purr creeps down the hallway from my bedroom, slinking through the manipulative curve of a familiar mouth, vibrating over the perfumed skin of a porn-star body.

Trying to let go of someday, honey? That's why you're so bitter about that beautiful family on the Christmas card. You had your chance, you know, if you'd only stayed in Seattle and given up the ghost. See what I did there? I always was funny.

I'll stay here, you stay where I can't see you.

You don't have to see me to know I'm right here, holding our baby. Wait a minute, we didn't actually have a baby, did we?

Stop.

That's right. I killed it. Instead of myself.

Her friend's eyes widen, and I follow her surprise to see my girlfriend, swaying drunk and naked under the arch between the kitchen and living room, repeatedly muttering *you cheating asshole.* I've been apologetically ushering out our dinner guest, and my girlfriend must be suspicious that in the few minutes since I've put her to bed, I've engaged in a momentary affair with her gay female co-worker.

I cover her with the couch blanket, guide her toward the bedroom, and after a couple of steps she spins, hits me with a closed fist in the cheek, and collapses in my arms. I carry her the rest of the way, her manicured nails scratching and fighting, until I lay her on the floor, where she connects with another haymaker and starts to cry. By the time I tuck her into bed and return to the living room, her friend has left a sympathetic note and shown herself out.

The next week, I break up with her over the phone, because I don't want the taste of too many cigarettes and too much chardonnay on her tongue, I don't want to live under the constant pressure of undeserved, presumed guilt, I don't want to get hit in the face, I don't want any of this as my future. Her sputtering response overflows with venom, infecting every vulnerability I've shared in nervous confidence, before telling me to fuck off and hanging up.

A few days later, the pay phone rings in the hall of my rehearsal space on the outskirts of Seattle. She knows our band practice schedule, and has called to tell me she's holding the knife and is going to kill herself, if I don't come to her apartment. I've already honored two of these threats in the last couple of days, bursting through her door to find her crying on the couch with no knife in hand, so I dial 911 to request a wellness check, and then 411 to get her mom's number.

Two weeks pass before my rudimentary flip-phone buzzes in the kitchen of a friend's house in Healdsburg, CA, where I'm on a day break from a West Coast tour. The number is blocked, but I recognize the voice immediately and step outside to the driveway, just in case the conversation goes sideways.

She casually mentions that she had an abortion while we were dating, but didn't tell me because she didn't want to derail my career, and she knew we'd have another baby someday.

That's all she wants me to know. The line goes dead and my phone falls from my hand, shattering in a million plastic pieces on the concrete, jagged heart shards glittering in the afternoon sun.

Come on now, why the long face? I told you I was sorry about all those mean things I said after you broke up with me. You know, about your mom, your music, your dick.

LEAVE.

Unless you're sad about this little dead thing I'm holding in my arms. I knew how much you wanted a family, but with all your touring and writing... well, you know. There's no time for a baby when you're chasing a dream, so I took care of it myself.

GO.

It has a name, you know. The one that got away.

I lay my guitar on the coffee table.

Elbows on knees.

Head in hands.

Wet eyes closed.

That chick on the spectral reality TV show made talking to ghosts look way easier than this.

BETWEEN A ROCK AND A STAR PLACE

I fall back into the couch and walk the canyon of wood grain along the fretboard, searching the fingered crevices for a place to hide from the glare of bitter truths. But there's no dark overhang to crawl under, only well-worn impressions made on small stages, where I can rest awhile in the familiar comfort of a song I wrote when I thought I'd be there by now.

The headstock of the guitar flexes in a *Fear and Loathing* warp, as a voice reflecting my own story, an inflection I've hung onto in massive outdoor amphitheater concerts singing songs that carried me through my early adulthood, floats in the air to my left.

Someone's having a pity-party.

How did *you* get in here?

Come on, man. I've been walking with you for twenty years, since that last summer with Jenny. I'm never going to leave.

Well, why are you talking now?

Because I'm tired of hearing this feel-sorry-for-yourself-nothing-good-ever-happened bullshit. Remember 14 Below?

I'm plugging my guitar cable into a tuner in a tiny club on a tinier stage in Santa Monica, beat down at the end of this farewell tour of tired bars and indifferent coffee houses, when two fingers in cut-out gloves float across my wrist. I lift my gaze and nod wordlessly in acknowledgement, incredulous that the familiar eyes twinkling under the dreads and woolen ski hat are here to see me.

He stands in the front row, a foot from the toe of my boot, mouthing the choruses to every song. This emotional, expressive voice, that I sang with one moonlit night in the heart of 20,000 fans, is singing with me in a crowd of 20.

And half of them work here.

A music attorney ushers me out to the parking lot immediately after the set with imperative what-if's and what-could-be's, and as he blathers on about what will ultimately not-be, I watch the dreads and ski hat drift by under the streetlights. A gloved fist raises in salute toward me, the attorney says *Is that who I think it is?* and by the time I sprint across the asphalt, the sidewalk is empty in both directions.

Empty, but for the precious remnants of breath left after a magical 7 songs, when roles were unexpectedly, unbelievably reversed.

Hey man, over here. On your right. Sorry bro, don't mean
to freak you out. I know you can't see either of us.

You're here, too? Sounds like that Georgia drawl is still getting
burned by a thousand cigarettes a day.

Ghosts don't get old, chief.

Are you here to tell me I'm full of shit, too?

Well, you did say that night at Eddie's Attic was sort of
a dream come true.

Five years after another songwriting hero's raw, inspired performance at the Paramount Theatre in Seattle, I get a call to
open one of his summer shows in my new hometown. His tour
manager is a friend of a fan, and later that night I'm invited to
perform on his December tour, and now Christmas is only two
weeks away.

We're playing at Eddie's Attic in Decatur, where he returns for
special homecoming concerts. I start my last song, eyes closed
heading into the first chorus, so I can burn this moment into my
book of better pages when I need someplace beautiful to turn.
The atmosphere to my right shifts, his baritone echoes through
my gut, and our harmonized voices reverberate into the sold-
out crowd that knows something special is happening to me.
He sings every chorus with me, following along as I improvise
a "Silent Night" finale, and applauds when I say *Thank you and*
goodnight.

And I walk out into the frigid north Georgia night, bowing my
head to whoever was responsible for this dream I didn't even
know I had coming true.

Do you ever turn to that page you said you burned into your memory?

Yeah, but then the reality usually sets in that I was only a speck of dust clinging to your shooting star on that tour. I could barely fill small venues on my own and sell enough CDs to pay for that night's hotel room. I was doing the best I could at the time, I guess.

Were you?

You think I wasn't?

You were constantly talking to a publicist, or music writer, or attorney as we drove from town to town. You spent more time on the marketing than on the art.

Nobody was doing it for me.

But it wasn't even the right kind of marketing. Those 'professionals' you hired weren't paying for your art, like a true fan would… you were paying them for a headline, which a true fan was probably never going to read.

I never thought of it like that.

You should've flipped that around, and practiced more than you promoted. I sucked at promoting myself, but I worked on my craft every day, which eventually paid off.

Hey, wait a minute, Georgia boy. You know that #1 song wasn't all you.

I know, I know. The four-letter word.

What's the four-letter word?

LUCK.

Luck?

Yeah. Some things are out of our control. Luck, good or bad, happens in that absence of choice.

You're telling me that his #1 song was because of luck?

Not only luck. You gotta make something great and work your ass off, but most popular artists will tell you that luck factored in somewhere. Unless they're ego-maniacs with no humility, of course.

What about making your own luck?

I think that's an Ernest Hemingway line. He was a hell of a writer. He also had four wives, affairs, paranoia, hemochromatosis, and an alcohol problem, before killing himself with his favorite shotgun in a rural Idaho cabin.

Point taken.

Look… some people write a song that could change a million lives, or a book that could influence an entire culture. But that song doesn't get heard by a million people, and that book doesn't get read by the masses, and it's not because the work isn't great. Just wasn't in the cards, nobody's fault. The artist's job is done if one person connects, even if that one person is themself. You don't need to be loved by everyone, if you're loved by the right one.

Spoken like someone who's already reached the top of the mountain.

All I'm saying is that not having commercial success doesn't mean your work isn't good enough. You should be making a life with your art, anyway, instead of a living.

How?

Create. Seed. Cultivate. Harvest. Repeat.

Huh?

Create the art and use it to seed, cultivate and harvest change in people, one person at a time. Nothing is for everybody, know what I mean? And change can look like a shift in mood, or feeling, or thought. Could be a dance across the living room floor. Anything, really. Then do it again.

You're saying I should've been finding my tribe one at a time from the start, instead of waiting on a record deal, or a manager, or an agent to bring me to the masses someday.

Not too late, you know.

There's hope, I suppose.

Hope is a close cousin to someday… they can both leave you sitting in the dark of dying stalks, waiting for the plow.

Sounds like a song.

Maybe, but hope isn't going to write it.

SCARS AND SEAMS AND SELF

As late autumn afternoons roll over to winter, the warm winds blowing west from the desert shift to colder gusts born over the ocean. The stiff onshore flow pushes salt air from the Pacific through the nature preserve and past this very bathroom, where the shampoo-tinged fog has impatiently laid in wait while I've been rehearsing songs, eager to chase the temperamental wind, desperate to hear stories of sailors and pirates and whales.

Opening the casement window allows escape for the overcast tiled skies and entry for a staccato melody. I follow the telephone wire strung between houses to a chirping finch, drop my towel, and wait for my reflection to take a less amorphous, ghostly shape in the glass.

A gust peeks through the window and the mirror finally loses its hydric veneer, exposing my bare torso and barer soul, stripped of pretense by these phantom conversations.

I hope they're over.

Pulling my shoulders toward my ears and back, I search for the correct Cotillion posture, ready to be evaluated for mid-life service. My left pectoral quivers, the steady drumbeat of my heart visibly pulsing under my skin. The notable layer of fat I brought home from college twenty years ago has long since melted into sinew, taut from solo surf patrols at dawn and evening sprints across sand dunes.

Most things you like to do don't depend on anybody else.

Hello, me.

Call me Alexander. Your middle name. In honor of Ben.

Ok. Alexander.

No tattoos, I see.

No, my only body art consists of these scars above my privates.

You hadn't been on the planet long when your intestines started bulging out. Those surgeries to put them back in were intense for an infant.

How do you know?

I was there, back before parents could stay overnight with their kids. You were in pain, you cried, you felt abandoned, and no one who loved you was around to help. Sound familiar? Emotions have memories, too.

Why didn't you help me?

We were both a baby.

Well, whatever. Nobody sees these scars. Especially since they're right above my privates.

People can see different kinds of scars on your face.

Those are laugh lines.

And is that some gray coming in around your temples?

Nah. Probably some blonde hairs.

Whatever you say. And is that an age spot by your left sideburn?

Whatever you're trying to do isn't helping.

Why are you standing in front of the mirror, then?

I guess I wanted to make sure I was still here. But now I'm wondering where the years went.

The years never left. They're right there, in your face and mind and bones and heart. You could refuse to honor them if you filter those creeping signs of gray out of your Match profile photos, and inject some botulism into those dimples-now-wrinkles.

I gave up on that Match profile hours ago.

You could also run needles and thread through the rest of your face, and delude yourself into believing that nobody could tell your skin's been stretched across your skull, like a bison hide strapped across a couple of two-by-fours.

You're not into cosmetic surgery, huh?

Remember when you started planning a river-rafting trip last summer?

What's that have to do with facelifts?

Tell me why you wanted to go.

A river can create the Grand Canyon with enough time, and I needed a lesson in trusting the process. But all I did was think about going. By the time I got around to booking the trip, snow was flying in the mountains and the river was frozen over.

So if you'd gone, you wouldn't have been floating anywhere. You'd have been sitting in an ice-bound raft, freezing your ass off in flip-flops and a Kenny Chesney tank top.

And your point is?

You would've been pretending summer, but living winter.

That's what you're here to tell me, isn't it?

You don't want to be washing that gray right out of your hair, and hoping that with enough needles and thread and products, nobody will notice that you're wearing stiff swim trunks on a raft buried in an ice flow.

Because *everybody* would notice?

Right. You'd be better off honoring whatever season you're in.

I think I'm in mid-to-late summer, but an early winter could be on the wind tomorrow.

Sandpaper softening splintered wood sounds from the bedroom, like the rustle of skin against cotton. Even in my one-night-love-affair years, I remembered if someone had stayed the night. Only tired pillows sleep over now.

I lean across the bathroom door threshold and study the tumble of blankets and sheets cocooning my nineteen-year-old self, tucked into a fetal position.

He doesn't know yet that Tweety never changed colors at all, that the real Tweety died when he was a kid. I want to warn him about what happens with Jenny, and tell him to stay away from that dinner with the drummer and the bedroom shade in Seattle. I want to hurry him out of town before the grunge hangover erases his confidence, before he gets too deep with the suicidal, manipulative ex-girlfriend and the baby they never had.

I want to read him this letter to my younger self that you're holding in your hands.

But I'd have to wake him up, and he looks so peaceful, so happy, floating on a calm sea of promise, somewhere behind his eyes.

Still dreaming.

MIX-TAPE

My jeans lose their protest against wet knees, and an excavation of the laundry piled on top of the washer yields a relatively clean shirt to wear, and another to lay across the guitar in my gig bag. I stuff the CDs I probably won't sell and the mailing list I probably won't fill into a backpack, along with a pair of socks, and my chargers.

Not Chargers, the football team. Their shitbag, petulant, spoiled brat of an owner, who inherited both billions and them, moved the team away, and broke my heart. So, I don't take the Chargers with me anywhere, anymore.

Both hands full, I nudge the door to the garage open with my hip, my first step across the threshold barely missing a mix-tape with I LOVE YOU written in different scripts. Braving the near-death spasms of the fluorescent bulb, I throw my guitar and backpack into Leia's bed and settle to my knees to hurriedly put back whatever else may have fallen out of the box.

You get tripped up by these memories.

Like cracks in the pavement. I thought you'd left by now, Jenny.

We're not done. And those cracks are more like potholes. You can choose a different road, you know. One that takes you someplace today, not twenty years ago. If you get out of your own way and let go, your whole world might change.

Sounds like you've been reading one of the self-help books buried in these boxes. Easier said than done.

Whatever. Doing something for somebody else is a good place to start. Like that.

Like what?

That mix-tape you're holding in your hand. I made that for you.

You did, at the end of our summer together. I played this tape over and over that fall, waiting on the futon for a phone call that never came.

The call came, just a little late.

I'm on another West Coast tour, chasing a barely breathing dream down Interstate 5 from Seattle to Long Beach, when the phone rings.

Jenny's done dreaming.

We meet for a beer a block away from where we'd had our first waffle-fries date. She tells me that when she left that message on my answering machine, she'd been on a meth bender with an ex-boyfriend. He'd pulled a gun that held a couple of rounds,

143

spun the cylinder, put the barrel to her temple, and kept his finger on the trigger, until she called to break up with me.

They call that Russian Poker. Russian Roulette is when you point the gun at yourself, which she was already doing with a needle and a spoon.

Jenny Cooper moves her beer bottle back and forth across the varnished wood bar, leaving wet contrails that match the single tear tracing down her cheek. She says that she's made a lot of changes, that she meant every word she ever wrote to me, that her heart was in every card, letter, and mix tape she ever sent.

I believe her.

The single tear falls, and in the quieted gravity before the drop hits the bar, I see myself.

I see a kindergartner in his Batman pajamas taking verbal bullets from elementary school kids. I see a 4th-grader at Cotillion who thinks nobody wants to dance with him. I see an insecure late-if-ever-bloomer afraid to ask out the prettiest girl in junior high. I see a freshman at a new high school hoping for a Homecoming date. I see an anxious college sophomore who thinks he'll never complete a defining rite of passage.

I see Jenny Cooper, my answered prayer, my dream come true at every turn.

And I never see her again.

Even now, I don't really see her.

I see everything missing.

The hope, the joy, the promise, the love, floating in a dreamscape of a decades-old dress, a beautiful ghost of imaginary thread, that no matter how hard I might wish, will never weave into the present.

The fluorescent light flashes once, in a last reach for life.

And I'm on my knees next to a cardboard box in the garage, concrete purgatory for what shouldn't be left outside, but isn't yet allowed in, clutching a mix tape in a calloused hand that once held the keys to an X-Wing fighter.

AN OCCASIONAL SHITBAG

And so ghosts have spoken, in hushed interior whispers, that the past is no yellow brick road sprinkled with the dust of gold fortunes, industriously mined by capable dreams. The past is asphalt, cracked and burrowed by faulty memory, trapping the traveler in bygone eras, good and bad, joyful and sad.

I walk this street in moments I want to feel more inspired, or vibrant, or hurt, or wronged, all symptoms of being more alive, falling blindly each time into an enormous pothole carved by a ghost of *Then*.

Tomorrow I may walk this street, see the pothole, and fall in again. But on my climb out, I'll listen for the echoes of a famed poem from a beautiful, creative survivor's soul. The reverberation will grow louder the next day when I see the same pothole, even louder as I walk around it, and silence into peace upon my choice to walk a different street.

But not now, because I'm late for my flight, which I'm blaming on the not-that-hot moms at Trader Joe's, although that was assorted spectral conversations and a mouse burial ago. Also, I forgot the travel snacks on the kitchen counter, so I stopped at the Mexican place in the strip mall for fish tacos. I guess the not-that-hot moms aren't guilty of anything, other than not being themselves.

I already have an indictable sauce stain on my jeans from trying to eat while driving, a mindless sibling to Facebooking on a steering-wheel-bound phone. Takes an occasional shitbag to know one, I guess. That may be a first, slapping a 'shitbag' sticker on my own behavior. I'm more accustomed to reserving that vaunted designation for the rest of the world.

Waiting at the offramp stoplight is a guy in a Vietnam Veteran baseball hat, holding a Sharpie-scrawled *Homeless and Hungry Vet, Anything Helps* sign. Will these fish tacos in my lap really help? I mean, will this breaded cod replenish whatever he lost fighting in the wet heat, only to face an undeserved, often more vicious battle at home? Will this corn tortilla build a bridge of compassion over the canyon of reprehensible societal reaction, spanning the gap between dodging bullets in the reeds and dodging batteries hurled by a misguided, entitled public? Will this lettuce ease the digestion of a dark homecoming, ever deepening the black scar that will be forever burnished into the conscience of this country?

A horn blares behind me, pulling me out of the monologue that sounds flowery and important, but doesn't change anything. This is probably not what Jenny meant by getting out of my own way.

I wave the car past me, roll down the passenger window, and

hand the homeless guy the rest of the tacos. He bows and tips the fraying bill of his hat, I nod back, and a few minutes later leave my truck in the short-term parking lot next to the terminal.

I weave apologetically through the airport security line, offering my blinking phone screen, as an excuse. Another occasional shit-bag move. The screening machine is giving a painfully slow birth to everyone's carry-on items, so I reach past the barrier and yank out my backpack. *Another* occasional shitbag move. I must have broken the seal. I'm shitbagging everywhere.

I launch into the river of humanity and ride the whitewater to my gate, where a serene voice announces the flight has been de-layed. I didn't even have to be the occasional shitbag I thought I had to be, because now I've got an hour of waiting.

Digging through my backpack, I find a book I bought last year in the self-help section of the Chicago O'Hare bookstore. I didn't need self-helping or anything, of course. But there was a picture of a dog on the cover, and she looked like mine.

I slouch into the closest chair and read long enough to figure out that these are stories and songs about real-life letters. A woman named Emily has sent a songwriter a letter, because she thinks his songs are pieces of himself he's giving to the world, and she wants to give him a piece of herself in return.

I used to write letters, too. Handwritten letters to Jenny, piec-es of me, which I carefully crafted on stationary, folded into stamped addressed envelopes, and dropped in the mailbox. I'd hoped she'd see that what made me different from everyone else, also made me special.

Special enough to be chosen.

She didn't choose me, though. She chose another hit of meth, in a studio apartment outside of Medford, Oregon.

We do some hurtful things to each other sometimes, which makes us do some hurtful things to ourselves, which makes us do some hurtful things to each other.

So I'm not sure anybody is born a shitbag.

Even an occasional one.

CHANEL

Fuck the 1%, taking more than their fair share. Know what I'm saying? I'm a Powerball win away from shoving one of these bullshit vegetarian sandwiches up their rich ass.

And we're off, on a culinary adventure at the Subway across the terminal. My gifting of fish tacos to the Vietnam veteran has lifted a lunch-sized burden from my conscience, but I had no idea such helpful social commentary would be included with my chicken and avocado foot-long.

I pretend not to watch as every third movement of sandwich artistry is interrupted by a demonstrative phone-scroll-hashtag search, ostensibly to gain her co-worker's support for a particular Chanel bag she's going to put on her credit card. Each celebrity donning the dyed-blue-leather purse is another nail in the coffin of $4500 debt, and social media's got the hammer.

Evangelizing pricey Chanel-bag life goals while railing against the 1% seems hypocritical, especially since she actually wants to *be* in the 1%, albeit via Powerball. If she won, she'd be shoving a bullshit vegetarian sandwich up her own ass.

Lotter's Law stipulates that this corner-cutting approach might not work. If she doesn't have what it takes to *become* rich, she's not going to have what it takes to *be* rich.

She'd enjoy better odds if she sets up a crowdfunding page for that Chanel bag, and assaults her fellow indifferent social media-ites with financial pleas that serve only her own needs.

There could be more to this girl. She might be going to school, or learning a trade, or working on a big idea, when she's not layering unrequested jalapeños on sourdough.

I'll take them off later. She's press-on-nails-deep in avocado right now.

She pushes the sandwich across the counter, oblivious to my cautious *Thank you.* I trudge back to the same plastic molded seat, where I settle in to unwrap her foot-long offering, and postulate whether this jalapeño-corrupted bread, chicken and avocado mash-up was worth eight bucks.

I guess I'm paying for her time and begrudging effort, too. Let's do the math.

$$\mathbf{B}read + \mathbf{C}hicken + \mathbf{A}vocado + \mathbf{J}alapeños \ (unrequested) + \mathbf{T}ime + \mathbf{E}ffort = \mathbf{8} \ bucks \ ?$$

This is no $E = MC^2$.

Wait a minute.

151

A glimmering diamond, buried for two decades under accumulating college silt, catches the light, as I begin to unwrap the sandwich art. I unearth the stone gently, removing each layer of dust with every tear of thin paper, and now I can clearly see the gem I missed in Econ 101.

Energy.

The professor spent half his lecture that day droning about daily life being an energy trade, powered by a cycle of choices to create or consume. Made no sense then. Makes sense now.

I trade my time and effort for cash. I traded that cash for this sandwich, to fuel the effort I'll trade tomorrow night for more cash. So, when I give somebody money, I'm really giving them a piece of myself.

Same with this sandwich artist.

Will she use her energy, her time and effort and money, to build a magnificent flying machine with rivets of determination and steel of sacrifice, driven by the jet engine that is her heart, so she can soar over whatever personal or socioeconomic forces hold her down?

Or is she going to keep dreaming of a $4500 Chanel bag?

I'm not surprised that I couldn't wrap my head around this idea of money, time, and effort as energy back in college.

I was still waiting for Jenny Cooper to call.

SMALL WORLD

I started taking delivery of a print newspaper last month, and stopped swiping right on my phone, for two reasons. The stories burnished in fiber and ink don't seem to be as knee-jerk as the perpetual inundations of small people lying to advance their self-serving narratives, and there's no comments section.

I tuck the rest of the sandwich into my backpack for dinner on the plane, pull out this morning's newspaper, and a headline catches my eye. Clearly I'm more newsworthy than I've been giving myself credit for.

The Year Christmas Died.

How did they know?

The first paragraph of the article mentions a directive from the Office of Diversity and Inclusion at the University of Tennessee, which orders that everyone on campus must ensure their holiday party is not a Christmas party in disguise.

Ok, this isn't about the mouse.

The directive includes a list of cultural symbols banned at holiday parties, like Santa Claus, menorahs, and mistletoe. No mistletoe? Sweet, now those poor kids are going to be getting laid even less than me. These college administrators and their yearlings that ban misaligned speakers are already anti-thought, and I'm starting to wonder if they know what fun looks like anymore.

I know I don't. Although I did love going to Disneyland as a kid. *That* was fun. *It's a Small World* was one of the first rides I could go on by myself, and I was in awe of all these different colored puppets with different eye shapes, dancing different jigs and singing in different languages. The only thing *not* different about them was that they were all puppets.

If that ride had been proposed for the quad at the University of Tennessee, an 18-year-old Walt Disney would've been subjected to this directive, indicating that he couldn't use any cultural symbols anywhere. And he would have had to ensure that he didn't use any puppets of a particular race, since he might offend a puppet of another race.

Actually, no puppets allowed, Mr. Disney. A non-puppet might be offended.

Small World would have been called *Suck World*.

The rest of the article takes a stroll down 5th Avenue in New York, where the holiday window scenes have bowed to pressure from powerful politically correct lobbies, and scrubbed away

Santa, reindeer, and anything else Christmas on 5th Avenue.

They left the Frosty Taj Majal, though.

Whatever. If a store wants to put Santa in their window or a college kid wants to have a Christmas party, they should be able to put Santa in a shop window or have a Christmas party. Or a Festivus party. Or a Kwanza party. Or a Hanukkah party.

I mean, just because somebody's circumcised doesn't mean they can't hang out at a Hanukkah party. I spun a lot of dreidels with Jacob Ross at his Hanukkah party the winter before the bar-mitzvah incident tore us apart. He was my friend, so we did stuff together. The best shit had nothing to do with words. Or directives.

And newsflash: Santa isn't Jesus. He's a fat dude in a red suit, delivering presents through a chimney.

I'm a little defensive of Christmas, the annual shining morning in my childhood when staying in between the lines was rewarded. This year, I'll be spending Christmas Eve in a sterile mid-tier hotel and playing for a handful of people misdirected into a club instead of a movie theatre on Christmas night.

After the show, I'll stare into the hotel room mirror under unforgiving lights and I won't see an NBA star, or a mechanic, or a woman, or President of the United States. I probably won't see Jesus either, which means some people have something I don't, and I have something other people don't, like the ability to write songs that fewer and fewer people are hearing.

155

That's what makes a culture work, but the traits that make each of us special probably evolved back when we ran in real tribes, not digital ones. I guess society is trying to level the playing field with these LCD policies. You know, make life fair.

But reverse-engineering reality doesn't work, because nothing about life is fair.

LCD *(adj)*
characterized by a bland, unremarkable result, as evidenced by the removal of what makes a human being or experience unique.
See: lowest common denominator. See also: parental celebration of mediocrity and societal push toward politically correct fairness

If life were fair, kids and dogs wouldn't die of cancer.

Bullies wouldn't hog the tetherball court.

And my mom would still be around.

ANONYLAND

I scan the editorial page, which is sort of like a comments section, except people sign their real names, there aren't hundreds of replies, and there's some sort of intellectual filter. Unfortunately, most of these letters to the editor are about politics and the economy, both of which rank high with religion on the scale of negotiable reality.

I leave the newspaper on the seat next to me and break my own rule by swiping right on my phone. My surprise to see a sports-related headline encourages me to click on the article, which celebrates the retirement of a female soccer player who's won a World Cup and two Olympic gold medals, and scored more goals than any woman in history, all while being an inspiring role model for legions of young girls.

And then, I make the cardinal mistake of holding hands with the Internet.

If you ever want to feel like people are total shitbags and the world is going to explode in a burning mess of stupidity and thoughtless idiocy, this is what you do.

You read the comments section.

anonyland *(n)*
mythical kingdom
where clever fake
names replace
accountability
and self-respect

A guy with *bagofdicks* for a screen name has
something to say, and everybody has a voice
here in anonyland, where nobody needs to
know your real name, so you don't have to
be accountable for your opinion.

Who cares, Fuck her. She should have retired years ago.

Did that guy get to the summit of whatever mountain he chose
to climb? I don't think so, because they don't have a comments
section way up there.

Way up there, they're *for* something instead of *against* everything
else, and too stoked doing awesome shit to say mean things
about other people's awesome shit. This guy is like a music critic
who tears down what other people create, without ever creating
anything themselves. Other than an opinion, of course, broadcast
via cockstroke, tap-tap-tapping with fat fingers that have to touch
a screen, because they haven't touched anything else for so long.

Axl Rose offered an invitation to critical bystanders before a
Guns 'N Roses song, when he copped a famous Teddy Roosevelt
speech about how respect should go to the man who's actually
in the arena.

*His place shall never be with those cold and timid souls who neither
know victory nor defeat.*

Axl's version was more to the point.

Get in the ring, motherfucker.

158

But that would mean stepping away from the digital keyboard.

Just because we can speak, or type, doesn't mean we should.

But everybody has a voice, right?

Including me.

Maybe I'm no better.

Fuck that.

I am.

Well, I'm going to be.

As soon as I get off this phone.

COUGARGARTEN

Not yet, because a bullet-laden question has been waging an unrelenting assault on my curiosity in untended afternoon foxholes. Ever since the brunette at Trader Joe's bragged to the blonde about taking an online course in manifesting, I've desperately wondered about the professorial figure leading these cougars into self-realization battle.

I took note of the name when the blonde asked who was teaching the class. And, despite my better angels, two clicks later, the thought-leader's painstakingly crafted face is telling me that today she's going to help me find my real, authentic self. She's the one with the perfect hair, perfect nails, and perfect lips, made up to the tits with every product on the shelves at Walgreen's, and she's going to tell me about how to be real and authentic.

If this is some sort of self-help story, somebody needs to write a not-so-self-help story for the rest of us. But I've succumbed to a masturbating chimpanzee frenzy, so I click on one of her social media links, which I regret almost immediately.

She holds up a piece of poster board featuring a cutout picture of a Porsche 911, surrounded by other photos that look like they were torn straight from the pages of *People* and *Us,* except for the pictures of her own book that she's sneakily positioned to sell her own shit. Apparently, this is called a vision board, and since the New Year is coming up, I need to get some scissors and paste and make one, to better manifest my dreams.

Instead of celebrating how lucky I am, I'm supposed to cut pictures out of vapid magazines, glue the artwork on poster-board, and tell my friends I'm doing soul work.

My mom took away the scissors and paste when I was five, after I affixed a paper light saber onto Tweety's wing in a team-building effort to save the galaxy. She pulled me away from the bird cage and took me to the park, where I found the most magical stick of my young career to bring home.

She told me to return the gnarled branch to the bed of leaves under the cottonwood tree, and upon my protest, answered with a concept difficult for a kindergartner to process, proving even more difficult for a mid-lifer.

She said I didn't have to own the beauty around me, like fancy cars or diamonds or sticks, when being grateful such beauty even exists would make me happier in the long run.

My mom got straight A's all the way through the Masonic home and into high school.

But she probably would've failed out of cougargarten.

cougargarten *(n)*
chardonnay-sponsored, middle-aged playground focused on false paths to fulfillment

MANIFESTING

The coup-de-gras, the raison d'être, the shining orb that has guided me here, is one click away. I'm about to take a cougargarten course in manifesting.

I've already determined that manifesting is for pussies, after spending way too much time on the couch, in line at Trader Joe's, and everywhere in between, thinking about *someday* but not *doing* anything, and becoming a pussy myself. I know, because I've seen my share of pussies.

Relax. I'm talking about cats.

Cats slink through the day pretending to occasionally give a shit, but most of the time they sit someplace higher, judging everyone else. Like that cat with the service animal vest, perched on the pet carrier over there. The only service that thing is providing is blessing us with her presence while getting a free ride, because her owner is exploiting a loophole intended for people who actually have animals that perform a service.

I doubt that cat is letting her owner know when a car is about to hit her, or when to take her blood pressure medication. Her life's purpose is to avoid eye contact in between self-grooming sessions, as she purringly opines over her immediate surroundings and ducks away from each passing, friendly hand.

I recently ingested a TV show about a cat whisperer who carries the tools of his trade in a guitar case and solves complex pussy problems in less than 20 minutes. Maybe he can help me, a little wizard kitten with a wand in my paw, sadly succeeding in my unintended quest to manifest my own shortcomings through criticism of everyone else.

The cat whisperer's shaved head and unfortunate facial hair live on *Animal Planet*, not this one, so I let the video roll and endure the introductory proclamation that manifesting starts with calling in what I desire, and imagining the feeling of getting what I want. But I'm not supposed to get too specific about what I want, because her friend thought she wanted to bang a tall black dude and ended up with a short white guy, and they're super happy.

Self-help? Sounds more like self-ish help.

She's ready to explain how to make manifesting work for me, when she demurs that she's not *actually* going to help me *now*, but she'll totally help me in the free class she'll be leading in a couple of months. She exclaims *free* over and over, like she's having a fake orgasm with Billy Crystal in a diner.

Well, *relatively* free. She rolls her eyes when she says *relatively*, like the absolute lie masquerading as an honest offering to a vulnerable demographic is no big deal, given the massive win she'll eventually provide for humanity.

Because all I have to do is buy her book first, and *then* the class will be free.

A reedy voice reverberates through the recesses of a 1983 hallway, when girls just wanted to have fun, time after time. I search "True Colors," and a click later Cyndi Lauper is reaching toward the moon, hitting a conga, and telling me in reassuring melody she sees my true colors shining through, and that's why she loves me. Her whacked-out hair and voice might not be what I'd usually consider perfect and beautiful, but they belong to her, and she owns them, which makes her sort of more perfect and beautiful. And she's sharing her truth with me.

I switch back to the self-help chick's video, and she is everything I'd usually consider perfect and beautiful. Long, blonde hair falling in carefully curled waves down either side of a meticulously designed face, shirt hanging sexily off one shoulder. But she's lying to me.

And this tinkerbell's schtick is starting to make me feel like I'm not whole, like I'm broken, like I need whatever pixie dust she's selling to be complete, like there's some one-size-fits-all-centerline where the gender-neutral goal is her: a sparkly diamond ring, nice rack, super skinny legs, and plenty of foundation to smooth out her perfect face.

tinkerbell *(n)*
individual who promotes fabricating false future realities based on wants, in lieu of assigning gratitude to the present moment

Not like my face, which is cracking apart from years spent running down a desert dream, under an unforgiving sun. I have cracks everywhere, in my body, my mind and my heart.

My favorite Leonard Cohen lyric says that cracks are how the light gets in, which I've extrapolated to mean that cracks also let the light out. Paintings, music, movies, books, philanthropy… real beauty usually seems to begin with something breaking, and when I started writing songs, I'd imagine that my own cracks were letting my light out into the world, a lantern glowing on a rocky peninsula for others fighting the storm.

How can this tinkerbell's light get out, if she's using broadcaster-heavy makeup, hair products and a whitened smile to cover up every crack she has?

Well, maybe not *every* crack. But she did expose herself pursuing her own greed, under the guise of helping me in this manifesting video. Are these her true colors shining through?

Or have her true colors been reduced to a dingy smog of half-truths and metrics, on their fight through the layers of eye shadow and mascara? She might put on this makeup, this aura, this pretense, to feel prettier in the barren afternoon of her own sand desert, as tiny grains of disappointment, eroded from majestic mesas of dreams and towering mountains of promise, slink between her toes.

As they slink between mine.

I'm listening, Cyndi Lauper.

I'm going to choose to believe this woman has a light inside, waiting to be refracted into true colors, beautiful like a rainbow, through the same cracks she's trying so hard to turn into cash.

She doesn't have to try *that* hard. Bleached blonde hair, half a shirt, and plumped, pouty lips should do the trick.

ALEJANDRO

I breathe deep amongst the urinals, finding lavatorial peace in the airport eye of hurricane holiday travel. A stall is more than I need, but I feel safer within the womb of metal partitions, less judged by the throngs of nobody.

I unzip my jeans and begin my emptying dance to the unexpected percussion of bristle abrasion on porcelain. A symphony of spray-bottling and paper-toweling unfolds next door, building to a flush of finality on my journey to the sink.

I'm washing my hands when he emerges, even shorter than me, khaki uniform shirt with the name Alejandro stitched over his heart, tucked neatly into khaki uniform pants, with a khaki uniform hat perched precariously on his head.

Our eyes meet briefly in the mirror, before he lowers his gaze and ducks into my former workplace. I silently ask the glass what cards Alejandro got dealt as an infant, as a toddler, as a teenager, ten minutes ago, but the reflection only shows how he's playing them now.

Spotless floor, shining urinal, sparkling sink.

Not only is this guy handling his own shit by doing an extraordinary job, he's handling other people's shit. Literally. Sort of like picking up someone else's bag of dog turd in the nature preserve. Nobody's ever thanked me, but nobody ever sees me.

I see Alejandro, though.

I wipe my hands on my jeans and brush over the twenty-dollar bill crumpled in my pocket, which reminds me of the AAA guy's request earlier this morning. Before Alejandro starts his migration to the next stall, I step toward him with the cash in my outstretched hand, and tentatively say *Merry Christmas*, almost like a question. Paying anything forward takes some getting used to.

He smiles wide with seven teeth, looks unassumingly at the crinkled paper, and back at me with almost wet eyes.

You don't have to cry, man, it's a twenty.

He shakes his head.

I nod and tuck the bill into the fist clenching the toilet brush. He says *Gracias*, I think *Feliz Navidad*, and a string of words I definitely don't understand. But I don't need to understand his words, because his eyes are glistening and his smile lines are deepening. He reaches out his other hand, trembling with small fingers offering a corsage on a never-forgotten Homecoming night, because his hand is mine is Jenny's, all holding a gift given, a greater gift received.

If my ill-advised brand of manifesting is for pussies, this is manifesting for humans.

MERRY CHRISTMAS

Is this where an ayahuasca journey or a supervised LSD trip leads, to the realization that self-realization might not be about the self at all? There's no need to spend the evening barfing up grain-free fig bars or watching spiders weave through manscaped pubic hair.

Just find an Alejandro.

On the freeway shoulder, or in the express checkout line, or behind the coffee counter across from gate 42, where a lady with a bright blue ribbon in her hair is telling an urban cowboy she likes his boots, and *Merry Christmas*, and some little girl that her stuffed Eeyore is handsome, and *Merry Christmas*, and an older gentleman that he looks dapper in his derby, and *Merry Christmas*.

I set my gear on the patterned low-pile carpet and sink into the chair closest to the counter, pretending to make deals on my phone, while I eavesdrop on her conversation with a co-worker about spending Christmas Eve alone. Nobody's coming to visit her, and she's not going to anyone else's house, because she has to get up at 2AM tomorrow to work overtime on Christmas Day.

I decide I'm going to buy a bottle of water with my debit card, ask for cash back, give it to her, tell her I like the bright blue ribbon in her hair, and say *Merry Christmas*. But I'm not going to do it right now. I'll wait until right before I board the plane, in case my idea gets awkward, because giving somebody money is a weird excuse to connect with them.

Money is energy, right? People give me their energy in the form of time or service or product, and I give them energy back in the form of money. I already went over this with myself. This is a way I can give her energy.

By the time I glance back at the coffee counter, the lady with the bright blue ribbon in her hair has left the cash register. She adjusts the water bottles one last time in the display case, says *Merry Christmas* to her co-worker, and takes off toward the terminal exit.

I fight with myself about whether I should catch up to her, regardless of not having any money, to say I like her bright blue ribbon. And *Merry Christmas*. I wouldn't normally even think of this, which is why I should probably, definitely do it.

I grab my backpack and gig bag, and fast-walk toward the terminal exit, searching for the bright blue ribbon. I'm a dozen strides deep across the invisible boundary demanding I go back through security, when a pre-boarding announcement for my flight sounds over the invisible airport speakers.

I sneak a peek at the TSA guy stationed to my right. He's lost in phone oblivion, so I retrace each step backwards, spin, and hustle back to the gate.

Thank God for the cockstroke.

FUCK YOU, INTERNET

The days of subtle deterioration were years, but the hour before she had to go, her bones and blood finally giving in, was a nanosecond. Strange how time slows in waiting, stretching into an elastic eternity, but retracts back into a single breath before an unwanted end.

Not like this flight delay, characterized by a very wanted end, and immune to an accelerated boarding process. The guy spilling out of the chair next to me sputters a drool-drenched *Holy shit*, and another, and another, which inspires me to glance sideways at his phone, where a cat in a shark costume is zooming around a kitchen floor on one of those vacuum cleaners that run themselves.

Whatever warmfuzzy progress I made with Alejandro threatens to evaporate under the blue light of my neighbor's cellphone screen. Salt tinges of bitterness erupt, as I realize this Nobel laureate and the 11,989,724 other hopefuls are Darwinian proof that the Internet most richly rewards the stupidest shit.

I'm forced to make a choice. A sudden, drastic pivot. Unthinkable, honestly. And while I bristle at the self-help phrasing, this could be what Jenny meant by letting go.

I'm Brad Pitt, on the verge of a long-gesticulating but never-imagined breakup. Internet, you can be Jennifer Aniston. Or Angelina Jolie, if you're feeling saucy.

I open the email app on my phone and hit compose, as the shark cat gives me a final push into an analog canyon.

```
Dear Internet,

Why do you like cats so much? People are out there doing
awesome shit, and you seem to care more about stupid shit
like cats in shark costumes.

Fuck you, Internet.

I'm pissed. I bought into your whole deal, and I'm not
better off now than before you came along, despite giving
you a ginormous chunk of my life.

I guess you've helped out in some ways, like making it
easier to buy airplane tickets. And letting me watch
movies that I don't want anyone to know I'm watching.

Hold on, I just realized something. It's not that I hate
you, Internet.

You do make it easy to buy airplane tickets.

I think the problem is more your hot stepchild, Social-
Media.

Could you talk to her for me?

I think she may be lying. Her name is already made up of
two words that teeter on the razor edge of surface bullshit,
```

173

but I believed her when she pretended to care about the awesome shit I was doing for her.

I knew better.

But I really wanted someone to like me.

And you know what?

She did like me.

Pretty soon I found myself doing shit just because I thought she'd like it, not because it was awesome shit to be doing. I took pictures just for her, I wrote songs just for her, I even shared my deepest feelings just for her.

And sometimes she liked what I was doing just for her. She'd give me a little thumbs-up, or a heart, or even a supportive comment.

But lately I've been feeling empty inside whenever I'm with her. I can't find anything to hold onto, because she's not here today, gone tomorrow.

She's here for a millisecond, gone forever, unless I give her a piece of myself again. Same as all the other girls since Jenny.

And I found out that it's not just my stuff she likes. SocialMedia has been cheating on me, because she also liked the art gallery opening whatshisname busted his ass to make happen. But she didn't show up, because she was suuuuuuperbusy liking the new album whatshername record-ed and worked weekends to pay for. But she didn't buy it, because she was suuuuuuperbusy liking the upcoming tribute at the VFW for nolongerhere, who fought for his country and paid for it with the rest of his life.

But she didn't show up to the memorial service.

See, Internet, most of the time your hot stepchild says

she's suuuuuuperbusy, but she doesn't actually do shit. She even told people to put the colors of the French flag on their Facebook photos, so they felt like they were supporting people in France after a terrorist attack.

She knew that slapping a grafickle on a picture with one click meant nothing, but it made more people feel good about visiting her, and she plays the numbers game. The more people she touches, the more gifts she gets, and the more personal information she can sell.

grafickle *(n)*
an image signifying mercurial, non-committal allegiance devoid of any perceptible action in the pursuit of real change

She's empty, opportunistic, and noncommittal, but sometimes she tells me what I want to hear, so I keep coming back. And she keeps comparing me to everybody else, but only everybody's best version of themselves, which makes me feel even shittier.

Because, dear Internet, that's how she makes a living for herself and that shitbag you married. After all, SocialMedia is really his kid. When LonelySmartComputerGuy met you, this was bound to happen.

So listen, Internet. I'm sorry about the F word earlier. This isn't about you.

If she comes home from banging cats in shark costumes tonight, please let SocialMedia know that I'm leaving her.

I doubt she'll even remember **my name.**

I leave the email open for a breath, before closing the app without saving the letter.

More for the sender, anyway.

UPGRADE

A human river clogged with storm debris lurches toward the dam, tree stumps of complaint and logs of entitlement slowing the flow to a petty slog. A few hundred years ago, this trip across the country would've taken a decade. Most of these shitbags climbing over each other with their massive carry-ons, hammering the frazzled gate agent with veiled threats, would've probably died along the way.

Instead, they get to bitch about how they're going to be late for dinner with their bestie.

The lady behind me is the only person in the vicinity not dragging three huge bags or whining about a missed connection. She seems Eeyore-sad, like the wind blew down her house of sticks on a rather blustery Winds-day, and nobody in the Hundred Acre Wood cares.

I touch the gate agent's hand as she scans my boarding pass, recoiling internally, because I'm not sure that wasn't creepy. Hopefully I didn't cross the #MeToo line in exploring a non-monetary method of connection. Impossible to know where that's drawn, these days.

I thank her for dealing with the grumpy passengers, she pats my forearm, says *Thank you, dear,* and a slip of paper prints out of the scanning machine.

An upgrade.

I'd like to credit instant karma, but I fly this airline whenever I can, even with unnecessary layovers and stops, and charge everything on their credit card. Sometimes the payoff is a bigger seat up front, which I don't need, since every seat is an exit row for below-average statures.

As soon as we're on the gangway, I ask the Eeyore-sad lady behind me what seat she's in.

Uhhhhhh… why?

Sorry, that sounds weird. I want you to have mine.

Uhhhhhh… why?

I'm in first class, but I'd rather not be.

Uhhhhhh… why?

Here, take my boarding pass and give me your's, ok?

Whoa. Thanks, man.

I lift my guitar into the overhead one row behind first class, wondering if I've lost what are supposed to be the best years of my life canvasing the country like this, asking people to like me. Which is another way to say *performing*.

I catch a glimpse of the seats in front of me, where some dude has his slip-on fabric shoes planted above the tray table, legs extended and crossed, with his hand firmly committed to the crotch of the lovely co-ed sitting next to him.

This guy could be one of those tech-no-life kids killing it these days. He looks the part, with his perfectly coiffed beard and gelled skull hair, unsurprisingly similar to the guy earlier this morning in the nature preserve, *and* the dude in the Audi.

tech-no-life *(adj)*
extremely well-versed in screen-oriented exploitation at the expense of organic experience, understanding, connection, and respect

The flight attendant is struggling to pick up the mess beneath the lovebirds before takeoff, and they make zero effort to help. The seams at her eyes deepen between sad and frustrated, as she surveys the tread grime streaking across the seats.

My neighbor in the aisle seat is watching them, too. When I catch his eye and raise my eyebrows, he frowns like I'm committing a crime.

Don't be so judgmental.

Sorry, man.

I shift my gaze to the window, trying to deflect the awkward silence that follows.

Wait a minute.

Wait one fucking minute.

I'm not sorry.

And I'm sort of disappointed in myself for even apologizing.

At first I'm talking to the window. Then I'm talking to the tray table.

And finally I'm talking to the guy next to me.

Judging someone's behavior isn't the same as judging the person. And if being judgmental means that I think leaving a bag of shit on the side of the nature preserve trail is lame, and cockstroking all the way through said nature preserve is lame, and massaging selfies until they aren't real anymore is lame, and driving like a douche-bag when you have a kid in the car because you're looking at a chick on your phone is lame, and being self-serving and ignorant in the Trader Joe's line is lame, and being an entitled helicopter parent is lame, and blowing through a stop sign on a fucking thirty-speed because you want people to think you're Lance Armstrong is lame, and saying Hit Me Up when you don't mean it is lame, and killing Christmas is lame, and thinking God likes you better is lame, and blaming the 1% for your own shit is lame, and comments sections are lame, and making a vision board with a photo of a Porsche is lame, and cougars trying to turn back time are sometimes hot but usually lame, and comparing each other on social media is lame, and disrespecting flight attendants while you're hammered is lame, and seeing all of this in other people means something lame is probably also in me, so I need to step the fuck up, then yes.

Fuck yes, I'm judgmental.

I pause for a breath.

The guy stares at me blankly for two blinks, pulls his phone out of the seat-back pocket, and commences the cockstroke.

Perfect.

I gotta go.

We're taking off.

TOOTHBRUSH

Plastic pull-down window shades shudder as the plane accelerates down the runway, asphalt rapidly escaping from the rubber tread. I prematurely ease my seat back and in retribution, the plane immediately loses momentum. The pilot crackles over the intercom with less-than comprehensive details about some mysterious blinking light in the cockpit.

Safe is better than sorry, folks, so we're heading back to the gate.

We deplane, and the gate agent tells us that we'll re-board as soon as the mechanics sort out the blinking light problem. Twenty minutes later, she says they need a part they don't stock, so they have to find another plane. And twenty minutes after that, she says they can't find another plane, so we're being booked on an early flight tomorrow morning, which means I'll probably still make my gig.

Leaving Leia in the metered short-term parking lot suddenly looks like an unintentionally brilliant piece of forethought. I'm going home.

The airline is offering a generous consolation prize of a toothbrush, a $20 restaurant credit, and a free night's stay at the La Quinta Inn close to the airport. The gate agent sidesteps the gathering line of now defeated passengers, and apologetically hands me the toothbrush and vouchers.

Sorry, dear.

I head across the terminal to the coffee counter, where I ask the new barista if he can do me a favor. I give him the restaurant voucher, which he folds into a napkin present, tied with a rubber band. He says he'll leave it in the cash register for the lady with the bright blue ribbon in her hair. I lean over the counter, watch him scribble *Merry Christmas Jenny* across the napkin, and offer my hand in thanks.

Two outlets down, the sandwich artist is taking off her visor and apron. I pass the hotel voucher across the deli case, and with a look of concerned curiosity, she hesitantly takes the piece of paper.

She can't have the toothbrush. Mine looks like a sandblasting tool for the mildewed tile grout in my shower.

WILDFLOWERS

Older light scattering through the smudged glass of the airport terminal strays in quality from an hour ago. A gift, this unplanned offering of hours, time I didn't know I had. Shouldn't this always be true?

I walk through the sliding exit doors and Leia seems surprised to see me. As we take a left out of the parking lot toward the highway, a Van Halen song comes on the radio, with Sammy Hagar singing about how right now is my tomorrow, which is some heavy shit for a guy who also sang about how he can't drive 55.

Except there's also a real tomorrow separate from right now, which is why you don't blow your whole load today.

So, he got that kind of wrong.

His book kind of sucked, too.

Motherfucker could sing, though.

I fumble with clumsy fingers through the center console for my *Born to Run* CD. I need to hear somebody who's been there tell me about getting out while we're young, how tramps like us are born to run, about finding out how it feels, and knowing if love is real.

My thumb brushes a cassette tape buried in the plastic case graveyard, and I glance at the spine, recognizing the small, careful writing as an astrological reading my aunt gave me years ago, for a way-too-young birthday.

I was bummed about having cancer, first hearing the news on the single-speaker Radio Shack tape player I kept next to my action figures. An effeminate, fortune-telling voice had told me that I liked to stay in my room because I was a Cancer, which made me re-evaluate my immediate future.

I asked my mom if I was going to lose all of my hair, and she said no, that I was a Cancer, didn't *have* cancer, and being a Cancer was fruit-ball talk, but having cancer was very serious and not to be joked about. These days, my mom is answering other questions, as her heartbreaking journey from knowing to not knowing, from never-before-heard *I love you's* to increasingly voiced judgements, from ever-earlier bedtimes to entire days spent safely inside, polishes a living mirror reflecting the seeds of my childhood.

Some have grown into cornstalk-tall briars, where I still hide amongst the thorns, highly evolved to protect against connection's closely related step-sister, rejection. Thorns of quiet countenance, of locked doors and dimmed lights, of conversations with myself. Thorns that keep anyone from seeing what's in here, thorns that keep me from seeing what's out there.

Wildflowers live in here, too, but they're harder to find amongst the towering dun of the briar stalks, neither planned, but both poised to spread wherever the other hasn't taken root.

Wildflowers with roots of compassion burrow here, sown by my mom's nurturing, thoughtful, and responsible nature, and stems of empathy, rising from the ashes of my deep introversion, into petals of music and words, seeded in a heart a dream ago.

Sometimes I'll dig deep into the soil, spread my palms through the dirt, and find a delicate root supporting a fragile stem. I'll gently work the wildflower from my earth, offer the piece of me through the weeds, and feel someone take the beauty from my fingers into their own.

But I hardly ever see their face.

I mean, it's dark in here.

EEYORE

Driving west from the highway and heading north up the coast, the industrial urban hardscape dissolves into a bastardly mix of dilapidated beach shacks and Tuscan wet dreams. The nature preserve opens to the ocean less than a mile ahead, and home waits on the other side of this bridge spanning the wetlands. I should be pulling into the concrete purgatory of the garage by the last verse in "Thunder Road."

Bruce is telling me to roll down the window and let the wind blow back my hair, he's telling me we're pulling out of here to win, and not to turn home again, and instead of hearing him, I believe him. I roll down the window, let the wind blow back my hair, and I'm not turning home again, I'm taking an abrupt left into the beach parking lot past the bridge.

I find a space in the back, open the door, and almost step on a dead mouse wedged in the crevice where the dirt meets the asphalt. The late-afternoon sun is framing every moment in such an impossibly perfect MTV light, that even I look beautiful in Leia's side-mirror, as I push my shoes off into wilted canvas weights.

Chris Isaak should be here, rolling around in the sand with that hot model from the *Wicked Game* video. Surfers are floating together in the ocean and lovers are tangled on the beach, and I'm not sure why I'm here, but acknowledging comparative loneliness isn't the likely reason.

I walk north toward the wetlands along the edge of the continent, matching each footfall with the retreating words that a sand philosopher etched where the water meets the land.

Is.

This.

All.

There.

Is.

A shriek pierces my brooding meditation, as a toddler to my left takes a frontal digger in the shallows. He's wearing an Eeyore t-shirt that says *Dreaming of You*, kicking at the waves, and screaming with the same joy I probably last let myself feel at 9 years old, mid-flight on Space Mountain.

The donkey on the kid's shirt billows and protests in the breeze, like he's trying to keep up with every buoyant, ecstatic bounce.

I can almost hear Eeyore groaning.

They haven't got Brains, any of them, only grey fluff that's blown into their heads by mistake.

We've been towing that same line for a while now.

You know what Rabbit said to me? "It's your fault, Eeyore. You've never been to see any of us. You just stay here in this one corner of the Forest waiting for the others to come to you. Why don't you go to THEM sometimes?"

Rabbit has a point.

We can't all, and some of us don't.

I've heard you say that before, too.

One of my classics. I've had a hundred years to change, and I keep saying the saaaame ooolllld thinnnng.

You haven't learned anything at all?

Well, I figured out that I give everyone a hard time because I think they could be living better. And I only think they could be living better because deep down I think I could be living better.

Introspective for a stuffed donkey, isn't it?

I know. I'm in my head a lot, which is probably why I started writing poetry.

Yeah, I do the same thing. I also know you can't read very well, which must make writing poetry hard. Christopher Robin showed you a wooden letter A, but you didn't know even what it was, right?

No, I didn't, which frustrated me. That's why I broke that wooden A into a million little pieces. It's okay, I wasn't very good at poetry.

What qualifies as good? People sometimes say they like my song lyrics, but that doesn't mean I'm not frustrated.

I think we're alike, you and me, and not only because we write poetry. We both get tired of watching people not being themselves, and pissing away the precious moments they have left here.

You think that's why I've been bitching about people on their phones in nature preserves?

Aren't you afraid that you're pissing away your precious moments, too? You see yourself in them. You only have so much time here, you know.

That reminds me of what my dad told me when I was chasing my music dream: don't be an old man in a young man's game.

Hmmmmmm.

What?

Well, I'm only a donkey on a T-shirt, but why would you worry about being an old man in a young man's game?

Just change the game.

189

BIG BROWN DOG

The toddler stumbles through the whitewater and into the arms of a smiling man with silvering hair, and they surrender to the sea foam wisps drifting south toward the parking lot.

Goodbye, Eeyore.

A thundering bark echoes from my right, insufficient warning for the big brown dog now skidding across my bare feet. She springs into a not-hot-yoga downward dog, eyes wide and focused with anticipation, her thick tail thumping a frenetic punk rock rhythm against the sand.

She tilts her head to one side and noses the air to my left. I follow her gaze an arm's length away, where a little green plastic fish rests on top of a seaweed pile. Sinking to my rump, I throw the fish as far as I can, which is about four feet. She leaps, pounces, and flings the fish into the air, catching it mid-arc before trotting back to me.

She drops the fish in my lap, but before I can react, she swipes it from my crotch, and sits down. I snag the fish back into my lap and smile, looking past her at the glowing orb in momentary repose on the horizon. The pause is enough of a window for her to steal the fish again and take off toward the ocean, leaving streaks of sand and slobber between my fingers.

I catch her before she reaches the water, pull the fish out of her mouth, and fall forward onto the sand, hiding it under my chest, until she lunges at me, her wet, searching nose pushing against my cheek. I give her enough room to find the fish, clutch it in my hand, spring to my feet, and sprint into the ocean, with her at my heels.

My jeans and gray t-shirt offer needed buoyancy in the waist-deep water, where she tackles my calves and sends me crawling through the shallow surf. We roll and fight and roll and I laugh and laugh and laugh and laugh, and I'm back on my grandma's kitchen linoleum with that little poodle before the kindergarten Halloween parade, living inside every single sweaty awkward special moment, as if this beautiful scene in space and time might never come again.

But now I have to stand up, because I'm face down in whitewater and need to breathe. I steer my teetering momentum away from the ocean and across the dry, soft sand, where I collapse with my back against the bluff, clothes soaked against my skin, shoulders and chest heaving forward in convulsions of laughter, interspersed with a futile search for air.

If I could find more of these moments, I'd string them together like photographs in a darkroom, each picture developing one after the other, moment after moment, day after day, into the story of my life.

That would be changing the game, Eeyore.

The big brown dog lies down next to me and stretches a huge paw onto my chest, with that little green plastic fish still in her mouth. I thank the sky, now tinted with orange and red and yellow, and let my eyelids flutter in a joyful, emotionally exhausted relief.

Only for a minute.

I'll only close my eyes for a minute.

POLAROIDS

I see a Polaroid clipped to a clothesline.

And another.

And another.

But I can't make out the images on the Polaroids, because I'm being pulled farther and farther away, until the clothesline is full of photographs holding together two buildings.

Hovering in dream suspension, I peer into one of the building's windows, where a guy is holding a phone with one hand and doing something I don't want to see with the other. On the opposite side of his apartment wall, there's a kid playing a video game on a tablet, the blue screen of escape and protection reflecting in his already world-weary eyes.

I follow the clothesline across the street, where a teenage girl is lost in the mirror, like she's staring into some sort of lonesome ever after, while a woman old enough to think she'd be somewhere else by now looks vacantly into the vanity, two thin sheets of drywall away.

I hear a deep bark and glance down at the big brown dog, spinning in circles on the street between the buildings. The clothesline pulls me closer, and now the Polaroids are pictures of little green plastic fish, moving around like they want to be free, but they're caught in the pictures and can't get out.

The dog must be asking for the little green plastic fish, and I feel like I'm supposed to help her, but I don't know how, which makes me anxious and wakes *Damnyou* in my stomach. I yell *Damn you, stop barking,* and she answers with a jump of countless stories, all the way up to the clothesline, where she snags one of the Polaroids between her teeth.

The Polaroid becomes a little green plastic fish, alive in her mouth. She nods at the next Polaroid, which I unclip from the clothesline, and the photograph paper becomes a little green plastic fish alive in my hand. Which freaks me out, so I fling it like a frisbee as far as I can. The fish flies through one of the windows and onto the lap of the older lady. She takes the fish in her hand, the apartment wall of separation dissolves, and now she's staring at the teenage girl.

I take down another Polaroid, which becomes another wiggling little green plastic fish, and throw it into the window of the boy playing video games. His bedroom wall fades to nothing, until he's within arm's reach of the guy in front of his computer.

I throw that guy a fish and he cups it in his hands and looks up at me and both buildings disintegrate, and now the family is standing together in the nature preserve down the street from my house.

They wave to me as the dog drops the last Polaroid at my feet.

And the guy says

This is all there is.

Weird, huh?

Whatever.

It was just a dream.

A dream about changing the game from isolation to connection through giving, from complacency to joy through playing, from someday to the present moment through gratitude.

A dream about how this is all there is.

But, like I said.

Just a fucking dream.

LITTLE YELLOW PUPPY

Warm, humid breath on my cheek wakes me, to waves breaking in rhythm with the slow, steady, forgotten pulse in my chest. The big brown dog is questioning me with big brown eyes, as a low fog, held at bay by the last lingering rays of sunlight, begins to creep in from the ocean.

My old dog and I would sometimes walk past the dawn drunks and junkies camped out against this same bluff, saved from the cops on four-wheelers by the evening high tide. At daybreak the winter before she left, she woke up a guy who said he'd seen 14 angels. I believed him, and from that morning on I started dragging her by the scruff past the congregation, so she wouldn't investigate what else might be bundled in those torn sleeping bags.

I've become one of them, minus the 14 angels.

Because these aren't the last lingering rays of sunlight, and this isn't some evening mist drifting off the ocean. This is the sunrise fog that rolls ashore this time of the year.

Morning.

I stiffly climb to my feet in still-damp jeans and t-shirt, and start the journey north toward the nature preserve and home. The big brown dog walks next to me, side by side, like what used to be.

Did you spend the whole night watching over me? You must belong to someone.

She abruptly looks to her right, ears at attention, and explodes into a wide open gallop toward a guy in jeans and a gray t-shirt, seated with his back against the bluff.

Must belong to him.

She throws the little green plastic fish into his lap, but he doesn't seem to notice. His shoulders and chest are heaving forward like mine were, and at first I think he's laughing, but as I get closer, I think he's sobbing. I don't like anyone else to know if I'm crying, so I walk past him, a little faster than before, and look the other way toward the ocean.

Maybe we're the same.

The dawn sea breeze seems to be building into a stronger gale, out over the waves.

Out over the waves

Those four words replay in my mind, set to a melody that resonates around my heart, a melody I know well, a melody I've sung many times, a melody I sing now, in time with my stride.

To words I wrote long ago.

There's a burned out Chevrolet
Out on the interstate
I left her halfway
When I found this little town
Started settling down
And selling out
Wondering what my life was about now
Living halfway
To someday

So I dreamed me away
Out over the waves
In that Chevrolet
Behind blue skies gray
I heard my angel say
There's no other way
From your yesterday
To someday
When you're living halfway

Chevrolet.

Shit.

I hope Leia didn't get towed last night.

I pivot to run back to the parking lot and almost trip over a small, light-colored blob spasming across the sand. On her final frenzied pass, I make out the pudgy lines of a puppy.

A little yellow puppy.

She scampers away to chase each receding wave with curiosity, before squealing in anticipation of the next one. I'm not that far from the parking lot, where she probably wrestled out of some new owner's hands, so I pat my thigh to encourage her to come with me.

She trots willingly and stumbles over herself at my feet. I pick her up, hold her at eye level, and for a string of eternity inside a single moment, I am lost in the pure, unblemished and unconditional love radiating from her seal eyes.

The kind of love the movies, country songs, and fairy tales say you're supposed to have with another person, in some beautiful ever after. I don't know, maybe some people are supposed to love a dog, or a river, or a horse, or a bird, or a mountain like that.

Like this.

Maybe I am.

I set the little yellow puppy back onto the sand, shove my hands into my jeans, and hustle toward the parking lot, now almost in sight at the far end of the beach. She alternates between jumping in circles around me and pouncing along the ocean's edge, like she's dancing to the song drifting through my head.

My fingers fall between foreign creases of paper running against the cotton lining in my pockets, and I pull out three crumpled photographs.

What are these Polaroids doing in my jeans?

Here's your ocean

Here, I'm on the living room floor, holding both a guitar and joy almost twice my size.

Here's your wave

Here, I'm smiling in a Batman costume, crouched over a small white poodle.

Here's your island

Here, I'm wearing a clip-on tie before that glorious last night of Cotillion.

Here's the way
To someday

The sinking morning fog has finally touched the sand when I see him. He's running hard, in jeans and a gray t-shirt, like he's channeling Forrest Gump's great escape from the bullies.

The crying-laughing guy.

Silver waves I rode
All the way back home

But the big brown dog isn't with him.

Where I awoke

She's gone.

Alone

The little yellow puppy whimpers as he passes. I follow her attention to the whites of the guy's wet eyes, but he doesn't seem scared, like he's running away from a bully, an unmet expectation, a decaying dream.

That same old house
That same old town

His tears shine with resolve, like he's running toward a new love almost found, a missing piece of himself to give, a fresh white-light tree to leave the gift under.

What he lost.

That same road out
To that interstate
There's that Chevrolet now
Take me all the way home
To someday

He glances toward the ocean, a million miles away, floating along the western edge of the nature preserve down the street from his house, where the dawn mist clings to the willows and a soft sea wind blows dove melodies from the cottonwood trees.

Here's my ocean
Here's my wave
Here's my island
Here's the way
To someday

His fingers brush the waist-high grass as he breathes deep and walks moccasin-quiet through the early morning peace, day-dreaming that instead of a reluctant warrior, he's Russell Crowe at the end of *Gladiator*, brushing the same waist-high grass on a battle-weary return home to his beautiful family.

Take me all the way home

The little yellow puppy whimpers again.

She knows him.

To someday

And she takes off at a wide-open clip, as fast as her stubby legs will carry her, toward the nature preserve. I'm not sure he even knows she's coming for him.

But she is.

I wish I could tell you what happened next, that the little yellow puppy found him in the tidal flat forest, and he rediscovered love, joy, and gratitude, the awareness of which is true happiness.

With trees and a dog.

But we're already gone into the cottonwood sunrise sky of the nature preserve, like two angels on the wind who were never really here at all.

GOODBYE

The first thing I remember about being on the planet is sitting in my stroller, which my mom was pushing under the Frontierland sign, toward the Walt Disney statue. I couldn't get my tiny fingers wrapped around the Cheerios in the stroller tray, so I looked at the statue, then up at the sun.

Disneyland used real paper tickets for rides back then, before E-tickets were reduced to Fastpass barcodes on cell phones. There were A, B, C, and D-tickets, too, but an E-ticket was the most coveted and precious of all.

An E-ticket got you on Space Mountain.

My childhood was measured by a yearly progression from my stroller to being tucked into a boat on Small World, to sitting by myself on Mr. Toad's Wild Ride, to coaxing myself through the entry hall of the Haunted Mansion. But I'd been too short for most of the E-ticket rides, so I never knew what I was missing.

Until the unthinkable, incredible, beautiful everything happened.

We were at Disneyland for my 9th birthday in the middle of the week, and Main Street was empty. My mom gave me an E-ticket, and I ran the endless miles of chain separating the non-existent lines for Space Mountain, before sliding to a stop in front of the futuristic sign showing the cut-off height.

I was still too short, by at least a couple of inches.

The unexpected devastation must have been written all over my face, because the ticket-taker girl with an Eeyore on her *Jenny* name-tag looked from me to the sign and back down to me, winked, nodded and smiled, and didn't even take my E-ticket.

She just pointed to the front row.

I couldn't believe it. The empty spaceship pulled up, and in my amped excitement, I stumbled into the rocket and landed with one knee on the seat and the other on the floor. I managed to get myself into a pre-launch position, but couldn't figure out how to get the seatbelt on, so I started panicking.

Quietly, because nobody was going to know that I was a 9-year-old Space Mountain virgin that had stolen an X-Wing fighter for the mission. And just when I thought the spaceship was going to take off without me buckled in, which meant I probably wouldn't survive this journey into unknown galaxies, hands with a face I never did see reached down, locked me in, and patted my shoulder.

I looked back at Jenny, as the plastic-metal sled lurched forward on the track.

She smiled and waved goodbye.

And I put my fists in the air, but not because that's what you do on Space Mountain, even though they tell you not to. I put my fists in the air because my whole life, all 9 years of it, I'd been too short, or too young, or too quiet, or too shy, and with one small, slightly-against-a-lame-rule thing, Jenny had made me feel like Rocky Balboa with his fists in the air and blood running down his face and the whole world at his feet after knocking out Apollo Creed.

About halfway up the climb to Space Mountain's first drop, I thought I should celebrate with a cuss word, despite the fact that my mom had shoved a bar of soap between my teeth the day before, in a futile attempt to clean out my filthy mouth, and wouldn't hesitate to do it again.

My mom would find out. Somehow she found out about everything.

But I didn't know the cuss word for this. What was the cuss word for joy, and fear, and anticipation, and gratitude, all mixed together? All I knew was that I wanted everything to be an E-ticket ride, and that I loved Jenny for making this small-but-every-thing-moment happen.

The spaceship cranked up, and up, and up, and I kept my hands in the air, even though, especially because, I didn't know what was coming. A giant endless night sky with stars and planets enveloped me, as I floated in that momentary release when whatever was pulling me into space finally let me go.

And then I was flying.

I looked at the sky the whole time. The moments I was scared. The moments I was exhilarated. The moments I lost my breath.

The moments I found my breath. The moments I wanted this all to stop. The moments I wanted this all to never end. The moments I couldn't think about anything else, couldn't think at all, could only be.

The moments I knew I was alive.

And I lived inside every single sweaty special moment, as if this beautiful scene in space and time might never come again.

I didn't cuss once.

I only knew one fucking word, anyway.

Disneyland, 9th birthday, sometime after Space Mountain

Kitt Doucette read this story and told me it could suck less, over and over and over, until by his estimation, it no longer sucked, and he disappeared into the great wild of his life's adventure.

I changed everyone's names in the story, because everything actually happened, and the world could use a little less Facebook-stalking. Yes, the photographs are real. And no, I haven't talked to Jenny Cooper since that night at the bar.

Maybe by the time you read this, Jenny and I will have reunited on a lonely street corner in our old neighborhood, wet tears lost in the moonlit rain. We'll be living with our Labrador and toddler in a converted Sprinter van, chasing every sunset and embracing every sunrise in the world's most beautiful locales. You know, #vanlife.

Or, at least I'll be a little closer to figuring my shit out and enjoying the time I have left here.

I hope you are, too.

ABOUT THE AUTHOR

Alex Woodard has toured nationally behind several critically acclaimed albums, earning a few prestigious industry nods while sharing the stage with some of his heroes. His FOR THE SENDER book, album, and concert series has earned praise from Huffington Post (*important, enlightening, and ultimately inspiring*), Deepak Chopra (*a beautiful tribute to the resilience of the human spirit*), Dr. Wayne Dyer (*an inspiring, thought-provoking, and life-changing work*), Ellen DeGeneres (*I. love. this.*), and Billboard Magazine (*one of the year's most touching, unique releases*), among others.

Alex writes, sings, and plays his way from the California coast to the mountains of Idaho, happy to share the pilgrimage with a Labrador and two horses.